BRITAIN
for
BIKERS

Simon Weir

Published by Geographers'
A-Z Map Company Limited
An imprint of HarperCollins Publishers
Westerhill Road
Bishopbriggs
Glasgow
G64 2QT

HarperCollinsPublishers
Macken House, 39/40 Mayor Street Upper,
Dublin 1, D01 C9W8, Ireland

www.az.co.uk
a-z.maps@harpercollins.co.uk

1st edition 2022

A catalogue record for this book
is available from the British Library.

ISBN 978-0-00-849629-6

10 9 8 7 6 5 4 3 2

Printed in Malaysia

welcome

Hello there. Thanks for picking up *Britain for Bikers*. This collection of 100 new routes covering England, Wales, Scotland and Northern Ireland is all about short, accessible rides – ones that can easily be fitted into a weekend morning or afternoon.

There are routes covering every corner of the country, so there should always be one quite close to you. If you have a whole day to play with, why not travel to a new area to ride one of these tried-and-tested routes? They're short enough that you should still get home at a sensible time.

At heart, these routes are all about the social side of biking. My biking friends have helped me select roads and refine the routes – and there's nothing so enjoyable as riding them together. I hope you'll use this book as an excuse to meet up with your motorcycling mates and go for a rideout.

Enjoy *Britain for Bikers* – and enjoy the rides!

Simon Weir
www.simonweir.co.uk

3

how to use this book

This is a slightly unusual book as there's not much to read. It's designed with one purpose in mind: to guide you around the routes in the simplest way possible. All you need is a tankbag with a clear map pocket, in which you can place the book, and time to enjoy the ride.

All of the rides in this book are circular, and they start and finish at petrol stations. This is because they're easy places to meet up with your friends if you use the routes for social rideouts, but there are a couple of practical reasons for this too.

It's really important to fill the tank up at the starting petrol station – and zero the trip. If you're in a group and everyone does this, you know everyone will have enough fuel for the route. Much more importantly, the roadbook uses the trip mileage to help you navigate accurately. Keeping an eye on the trip helps keep you on the route.

Using the map

If you want to follow the route on the map, please take the time to study it first. If you have the route roughly in your head before starting the ride, you can confirm directions with a glance at the map as you go.

Never look away from the road for an extended length of time. If you need to study the map – if you think you've missed a turning and gone astray – find a safe place to stop and check it.

Using the roadbook

If you want to follow the route by using the directions in the roadbook, please study the map before setting off. You should have a good idea of the route in your head, so you can absorb the next direction from the roadbook at a glance: never ride along staring at it. If you become unsure, find a safe place to stop to check the map and directions.

Starting station: Esso, King Street, Weymouth DT4 7BJ

MILE	LOCATION	TURN	ON	TO	FOR
0	Weymouth	↰ ↑	B3155	**Overcombe**	2.5
2.5	Overcombe	↔◇⚲	A353	**Preston**	4.5
7	Warmwell Cross	⚲	B3390	**Affpuddle**	7.5
14.5	A35	↰	minor	**Tolpuddle**	4
18.5	Puddletown	⮆	A354	**All routes**	0.5
19	A35	↰	B3142	**Piddlehinton**	2.5

There are six columns in the roadbook: **MILE**, **LOCATION**, **TURN**, **ON**, **TO**, **FOR**.

The **MILE** column shows – to the nearest half mile – when you need to make a turn after leaving the starting petrol station. This is why it's crucial to zero the trip there before setting off. If it says, for example, at mile 12.5 you will need to turn left, start looking for the turning when you have 12 miles on your trip.

The **LOCATION** column gives you a more general area for the turning – whether it's a town or a junction. If it's just a road number, that indicates you'll be turning off the road. This is where the **MILE** column and your trip will help you find the right turning.

When you're on one road, stay with it until the directions tell you to turn. For ambiguous junctions – staggered crossroads, major roundabouts, etc – there may be a specific direction to go straight ahead. For any minor junctions, just go straight ahead – the roadbook will confirm, with the trip mileage, when to turn onto a new road.

The **TURN** column shows which way to go. Just to confirm, left is this symbol ⬑ – and right is this symbol ⬏. With roundabouts and double roundabouts, the icon reflects the exit you need to take.

If you're at a point where you need to make two turns within 400 to 500 m of each other – say, turning left out of the initial petrol station and then right at the roundabout at the end of the road – there will be two symbols in this column.

The **ON** column shows the road number of the road you're turning onto. If it's a small road without a number, it will just say 'minor'.

The **TO** column shows the name you'll see on the road sign at the junction where you turn.

The **FOR** column shows how far you need to ride to the next turn. Glance at it once you've made the turn… just in case it's only half a mile to the next turn.

Reading roadbooks well does take practice. I'd recommend keeping a conservative pace at first as the most important thing is to concentrate on the road at all times. If in doubt, stop to check the map. There's no harm in making a turn and then pulling in for two seconds to double-check the directions for the next leg of the route. But if you keep an eye on your trip and the turn directions, it's easy enough.

Using a sat nav
If your bike is fitted with a sat nav, or if you have a phone holder and use a smartphone navigation app like Calimoto or Scenic, you can either use the maps in the book to help you plot the route or you can download a GPX file for any route from: www.simonweir.co.uk

Group riding
These routes will work for solo riders or small groups – and really, the idea of the book is to give an excuse to get the gang together for a slightly different rideout to the usual ones. So here are a few notes on group riding.

Most importantly, give each other a bit of space. Ride in an off-set, staggered formation on the straights and, approaching corners, adjust your speed to spread out so everyone not only gets to take the best line but also has the time to read the bends properly.

Don't do group overtakes – assess each opportunity for yourself, as a safe pass for the leading rider might be downright scary for the one at the back. Be cautious if catching a queue of traffic, in case the vehicle at the front is about to turn right…

Keep the group together – even if you think the leader's gone astray, don't detonate the group by just riding off in a different direction. Equally, don't turn off a road unless you can see the rider behind you – try to wait safely at the junction if they need to catch up.

Perhaps the two most important bits of advice would be: make sure everyone has each other's phone numbers, so you can use your mobiles if you do get split up; and… just relax, ride safely and have fun.

guide to roadbook symbols

Junctions and turns
left, right and straight on

Crossroads
left, right and straight on

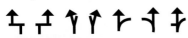

Junctions and turns
more complicated, road layout reflects
what you will encounter

Roundabouts
left, right and straight on

Mini-roundabouts
left, right and straight on

Roundabouts and mini-roundabouts
more complicated, road layout reflects what
you will encounter, some examples only

Traffic lights
left, right and straight on

Traffic lights
more complicated, road layout reflects
what you will encounter

Ferry crossing

contents

England – South and Southwest

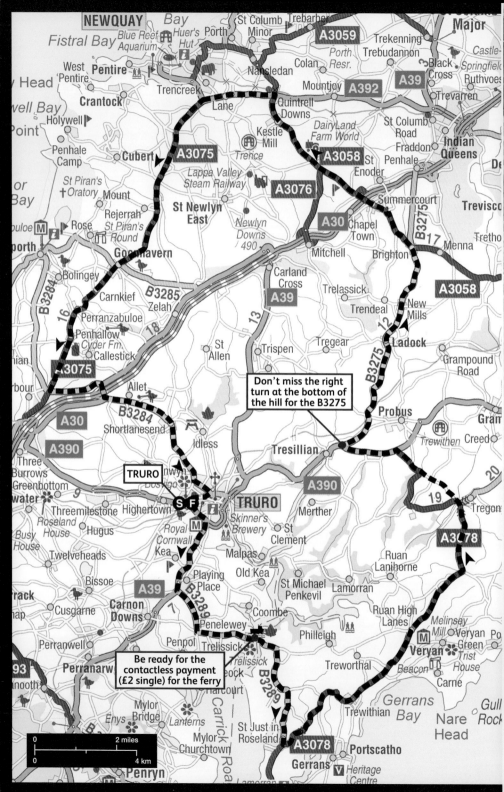

1 Cornish Cream

Cornwall can be a magical place – but it can be busy, especially at the coast. Though this route passes holiday hotspot Newquay, it largely uses quieter inland roads.

FROM	Truro
DISTANCE	48.5 miles
ALLOW	1 hr 20 mins

Starting station: Sainbury's, Treyew Road, Truro TR1 3XL

MILE	LOCATION	TURN	ON	TO	FOR
0	Truro		A390	**St Austell**	1
1	Truro		A39	**Falmouth**	2
3	Playing Place		B3289	**St Mawes**	2.5
5.5	King Harry ferry		B3289	**St Mawes**	3
8.5	St Just in Roseland		A3078	**Truro**	11.5
20	A390 T-junction		A390	**Truro**	1.5
21.5	A390		B3275	**Ladock**	5.5
27	Brighton Cross		A3058	**Newquay**	5.5
32.5	Quintrell Downs		A392	**Newquay**	2
34.5	Newquay		A3075	**Redruth**	8
42.5	Pendown Cross		B3284	**Truro**	1
43.5	A30		B3284	**Truro**	5
48.5	Truro				

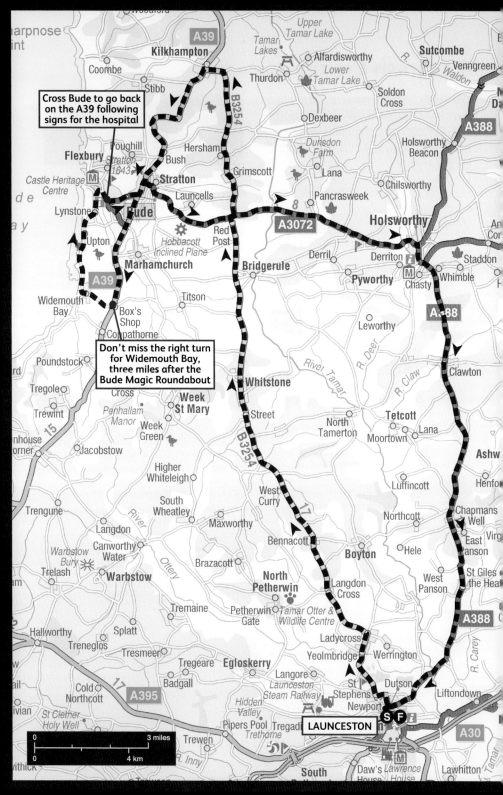

Cross Bude to go back on the A39 following signs for the hospital

Don't miss the right turn for Widemouth Bay, three miles after the Bude Magic Roundabout

LAUNCESTON

2 Launceston Triple Loop

This cat's cradle of a route is easily adapted if you need a quicker ride: just hang a right at the Red Post Inn on the A3072 – but that means missing out on Widemouth Bay.

FROM	Launceston
DISTANCE	53 miles
ALLOW	1 hr 20 mins

Starting station: BP, Newport Square, Launceston PL15 8DF

MILE	LOCATION	TURN	ON	TO	FOR
0	Launceston		B3254	**Bude**	14.5
14.5	Red Post Inn		B3254	**Kilkhampton**	4.5
19	Kilkhampton		A39	**Bude**	7
26	A39		minor	**Widemouth Bay**	1
27	Widemouth Bay		minor	**Bude**	4
31	Bude		A39	**Bideford**	0.5
31.5	Bude		A3072	**Holsworthy**	8
39.5	Holsworthy		A388	**Launceston**	13.5
53	Launceston				

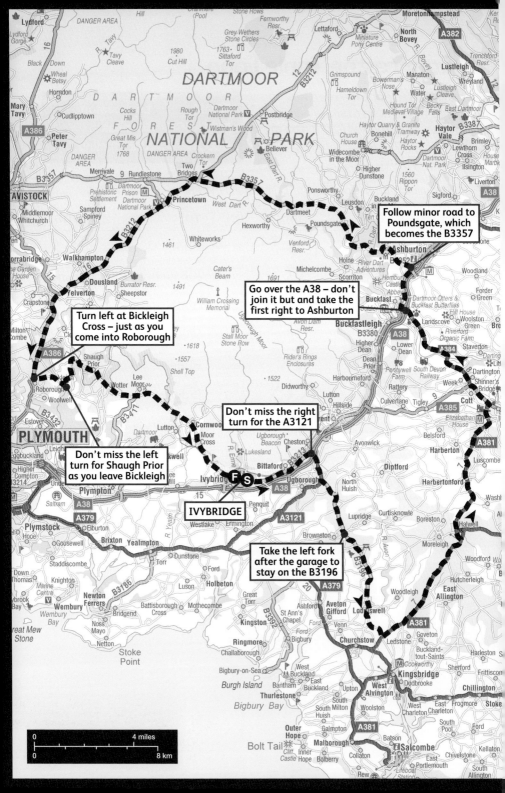

Follow minor road to Poundsgate, which becomes the B3357

Go over the A38 – don't join it but and take the first right to Ashburton

Turn left at Bickleigh Cross – just as you come into Roborough

Don't miss the right turn for the A3121

Don't miss the left turn for Shaugh Prior as you leave Bickleigh

IVYBRIDGE

Take the left fork after the garage to stay on the B3196

3 Dartmoor and More

I'm not a big fan of the A38. It's an efficient enough road, I guess, but I prefer the minor roads around it – especiallly as they lead to the untamed beauty of Dartmoor. On a sunny day, it's close to heaven.

FROM	Ivybridge
DISTANCE	65 miles
ALLOW	1 hr 45 mins

Starting station: BP, Leonards Road, Ivybridge PL21 0RU

MILE	LOCATION	TURN	ON	TO	FOR
0	Ivybridge	↱ ⟳	B3213	**Bittaford**	3.5
3.5	B3213	↱	A3121	**Ugborough**	1
4.5	Kitterford Cross	✛	B3196	**Loddiswell**	2.5
7	California Cross	↑	B3196	**Loddiswell**	5
12	Sorley Green Cross	↰	A381	**Totnes**	11.5
23.5	Totnes	◀🚦	A385	**Exeter**	1
24.5	Dartington	⟳	A384	**Ashburton**	4.5
29	A38 flyover	↱	minor	**Ashburton**	1.5
30.5	Shell garage	↰	minor	**Poundsgate**	11.5
42	Two Bridges	↰	B3212	**Princetown**	7
49	Yelverton	⟲	A386	**Plymouth**	4
53	Roborough	↰	minor	**Bickleigh**	1
54	Bickleigh	↰	minor	**Shaugh Prior**	11
65	Ivybridge				

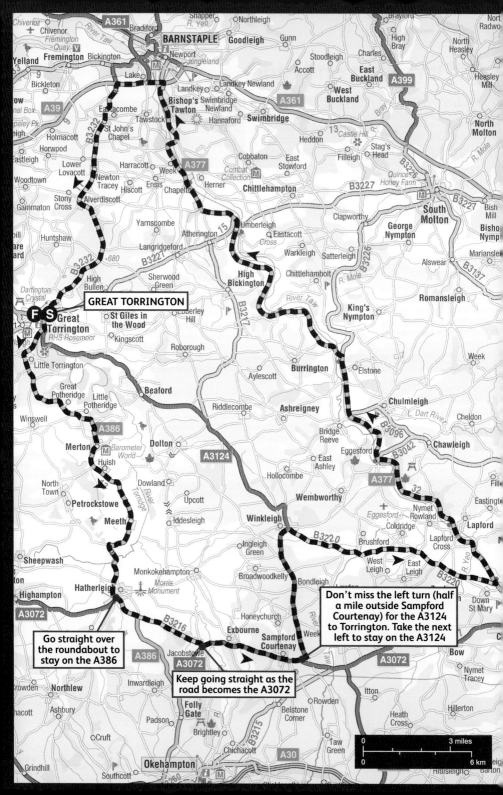

4 Torrington Triangle

The West Country often seems to be pretty extreme, with the roads either empty or full, never a little busy but not too bad... or maybe that's just when I visit. This route is stunning on one of those empty days.

FROM	Great Torrington
DISTANCE	68 miles
ALLOW	1 hr 30 mins

Starting station: BP, New Road, Great Torrington EX38 8EJ

MILE	LOCATION	TURN	ON	TO	FOR
0	Great Torrington	⬑	A386	**Okehampton**	13.5
13.5	Basset's Cross	⬈	B3216	**Winkleigh**	6
19.5	A3072	⬑ ⬑	A3124	**Torrington**	5
24.5	Winkleigh	⬏	B3220	**Exeter**	8
32.5	A377 junction	⬑	A377	**Barnstaple**	25
57.5	Barnstaple	⬅◯➡	A361	**Bideford (A39)**	0.5
58	Barnstaple	⬆◯	A39	**Bideford**	1
59	Barnstaple	⬅◯➡	B3232	**Torrington**	9
68	Great Torrington				

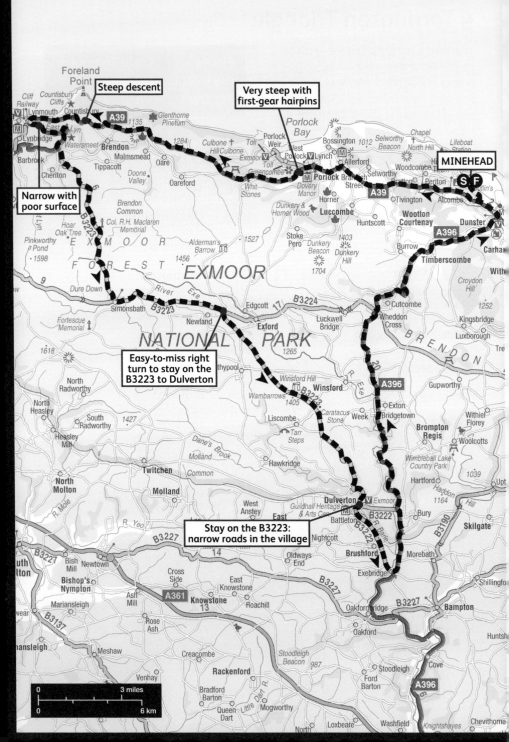

5 Exmoor and More

I love the A39 – it's wild, scenic and packed with great bends and awesome hills as it flows along beside the sea. Better still, it links with the far quieter B3223 that crosses Exmoor away from the coast. A great ride.

FROM	Minehead
DISTANCE	63.5 miles
ALLOW	1 hr 30 mins

Starting station: Tesco, Seaward Way, Minehead TA24 5BY

MILE	LOCATION	TURN	ON	TO	FOR
0	Minehead	↱ ⟳→	A39	**Alcombe**	20.5
20.5	Lynton	↰	B3223	**Simonsbath**	10.5
31	B3223	↱	B3223	**Withypool**	13.5
44.5	Exebridge	↰	A396	**Minehead**	17.5
62	Dunster	↰	A39	**Minehead**	1.5
63.5	Minehead				

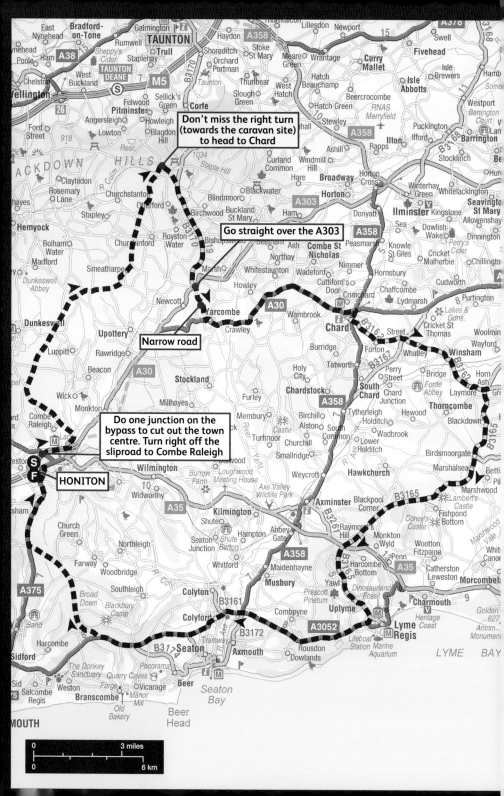

6 Honiton Loop

There are quite a few minor roads on this laid-back loop from Honiton down to the coast at Lyme Regis. It's well worth stopping in the resort for a coffee by the Cobb.

FROM	Honiton
DISTANCE	61 miles
ALLOW	1 hr 30 mins

Starting station: BP, Turks Head Lane, Honiton EX14 1BQ

MILE	LOCATION	TURN	ON	TO	FOR
0	Honiton	↱	A30	**Chard**	1.5
1.5	Honiton bypass	↰	minor	**Poole**	200 m
1.5	sliproad	↱	minor	**Combe Raleigh**	11
12.5	T-junction	↰	minor	**Blagdon**	1.5
14	minor road	↱	minor	**Chard**	1
15	B3170 T-junction	↱	B3170	**Honiton**	5
20	A30 T-junction	↰	A30	**Chard**	6
26	Chard	↱ ↱	A358	**Axminster**	0.5
26.5	Chard	↰	B3162	**Forton**	2
28.5	B3167 T-junction	↰ ↱	B3162	**Winsham**	3.5
32	crossroads	↔	B3165	**Axminster**	8.5
40.5	A35	↑	B3165	**Lyme Regis**	3
43.5	Lyme Regis	↱	A3052	**Exeter**	10
53.5	A3052	↱	minor	**Ottery St Mary**	4.5
58	Putts Corner	↱	A375	**Honiton**	3
61	Honiton				

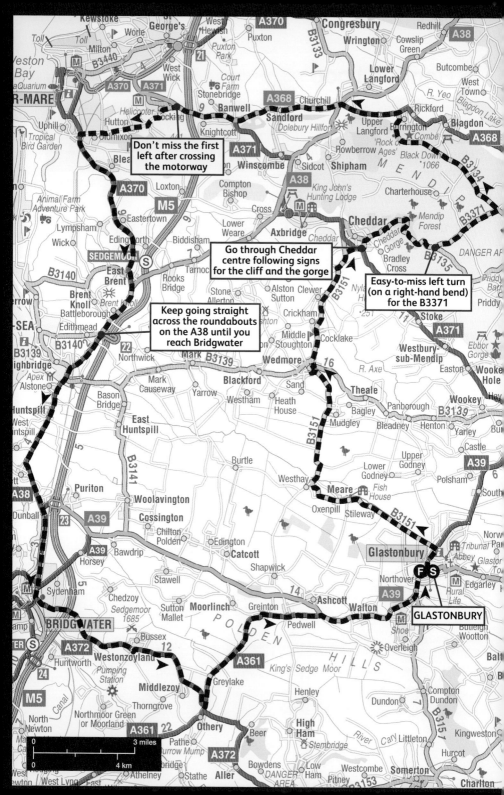

7 Tor, Gorge and Combe

This route around Glastonbury is another that's about timing: Cheddar Gorge and Burrington Combe can be spectacular... or busy. This route is still fun at the weekends, but try a midweek afternoon to enjoy it when it's quiet.

FROM	Glastonbury
DISTANCE	65 miles
ALLOW	2 hrs

Starting station: Esso, Wirral Park Road, Glastonbury BA6 9EE

MILE	LOCATION	TURN	ON	TO	FOR
0	Glastonbury	⟵⊙ ⊙	A39	**Wells**	1
1	Glastonbury	⟵⊙	B3151	**Godney**	8
9	Wedmore	⤷ ⤶	B3151	**Cheddar**	4
13	Cheddar	⤷ ⤶	B3135	**The Cliffs**	4
17	B3135	⤶	B3371	**Burrington**	2
19	crossroads	⟵╂	B3134	**Burrington**	4.5
23.5	A368 T-junction	⤶	A368	**Weston-s-Mare**	6.5
30	Weston-s-Mare	⤶	minor	**Elborough**	3.5
33.5	Weston-s-Mare	⟵⊙	A370	**Taunton / M5 South**	5.5
39	A38 roundabout	⊙	A38	**Highbridge**	10
49	Bridgwater	⟵▯	A372	**Langport**	7
56	Othery	⤶	A361	**Glastonbury**	9
65	Glastonbury				

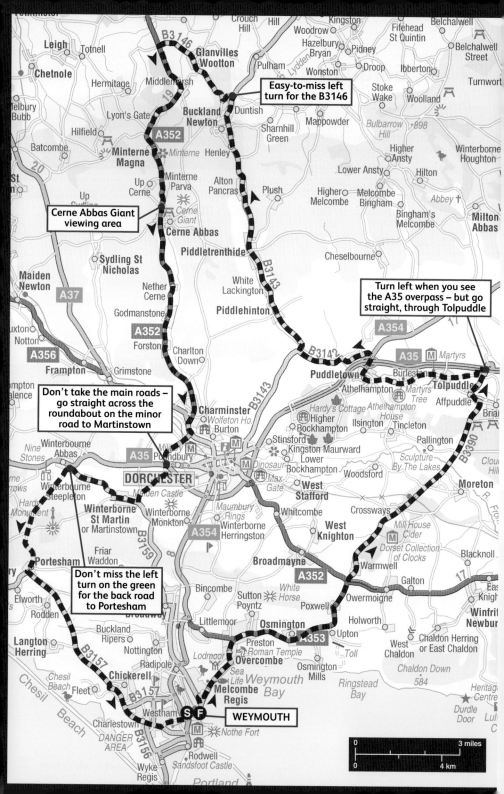

8 Weymouth Giant Run

No, there isn't a giant in Weymouth, but there is in Cerne Abbas. This relaxed rideout heads inland to visit the old chap, using some of my favourite South Coast B-roads.

FROM	Weymouth
DISTANCE	60 miles
ALLOW	1 hr 45 mins

Starting station: Esso, King Street, Weymouth DT4 7BJ

MILE	LOCATION	TURN	ON	TO	FOR
0	Weymouth		B3155	**Overcombe**	2.5
2.5	Overcombe		A353	**Preston**	4.5
7	Warmwell Cross		B3390	**Affpuddle**	7.5
14.5	A35		minor	**Tolpuddle**	4
18.5	Puddletown		A354	**All routes**	0.5
19	A35		B3142	**Piddlehinton**	2.5
21.5	T-junction		B3143	**Piddlehinton**	7
28.5	T-Junction		B3143	**Sturminster**	0.5
29	B3143		B3146	**Sherborne**	3.5
32.5	crossroads		A352	**Dorchester**	11.5
44	A37 T-junction		A37	**Dorchester**	1.5
45.5	roundabout		minor	**Martinstown**	1.5
47	T-junction		B3159	**Winterborne**	2.5
49.5	Winterborne		minor	**Portesham**	3.5
53	Portesham		B3157	**Weymouth**	7
60	Weymouth				

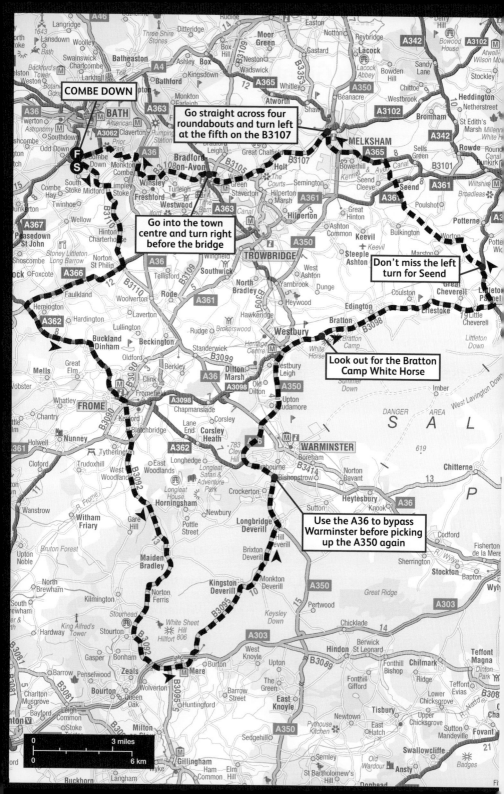

9 Bath Time

I love Bath – but the city's a congestion nightmare. So this relaxed afternoon's ride starts from the suburb of Combe Down, heading out to the Bratton Camp White Horse and lovely Bradford-on-Avon.

FROM	Combe Down
DISTANCE	74 miles
ALLOW	2 hrs 15 mins

Starting station: Esso, 100 Midford Road, Combe Down, Bath BA2 5RU

MILE	LOCATION	TURN	ON	TO	FOR
0	Combe Down		B3110	**Midford**	5
5	Norton St Philip		A366	**Radstock**	4
9	Terry Hill		A362	**Frome**	5.5
14.5	Frome		A362	**All other routes**	0.5
15	Frome		B3092	**Maiden Bradley**	12.5
27.5	Mere		B3095	**The Deverills**	7
34.5	Longbridge Deverill		A350	**Warminster**	8
42.5	Westbury		B3098	**Bratton**	8.5
51	Littleton Panell		A360	**Devizes**	1.5
52.5	A360		minor	**Seend**	6
58.5	A365 T-junction		A365	**Melksham**	2
60.5	Melksham		A350	**Chippenham**	1
61.5	Melksham		B3107	**Bradford-on-Avon**	5.5
67	Bradford-on-Avon		B3108	**Winsley**	5
72	A36 T-junction		minor	**Monkton Combe**	0.5
72.5	Brassknocker Hill		minor	**Combe Down**	1.5
74	Combe Down				

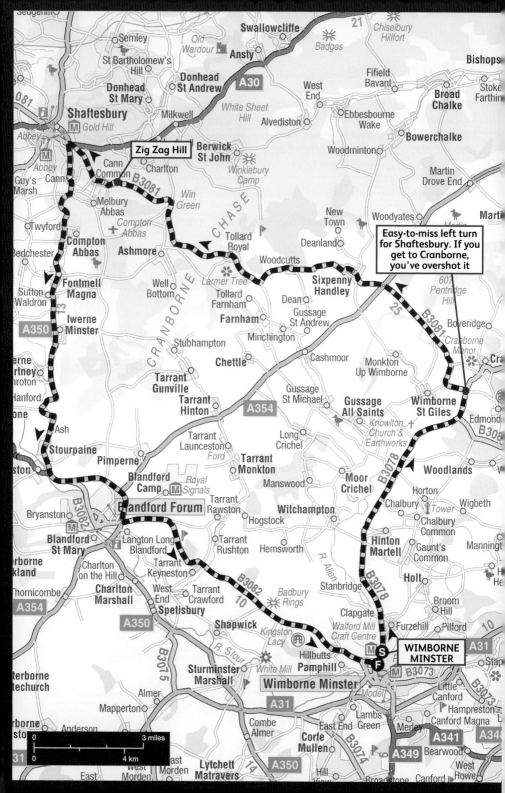

10 Wimborne to Run

This route is largely built around two roads: the B3081 over Zig Zag Hill, with its hairpins; and the A350 – which is a stunning road when it's quiet. If you can ride it midweek, you're likely to have a better run.

FROM	Wimborne Minster
DISTANCE	46 miles
ALLOW	1 hr 15 mins

Starting station: BP, Wimborne Road, Wimborne Minster BH21 1NW

MILE	LOCATION	TURN	ON	TO	FOR
0	Wimborne Minster	↱	B3078	**Cranborne**	8.5
8.5	B3078	↰	B3081	**Shaftesbury**	0.5
9	T-junction	↱	B3081	**Shaftesbury**	3.5
12.5	A354 roundabout	⟳	B3081	**Shaftesbury**	10.5
23	T-junction	↱	B3081	**Warminster**	1
24	Shaftesbury	↰ ⟲	A350	**Poole**	13
37	Blandford bypass	⟲	B3082	**Wimborne**	9
46	Wimborne Minster				

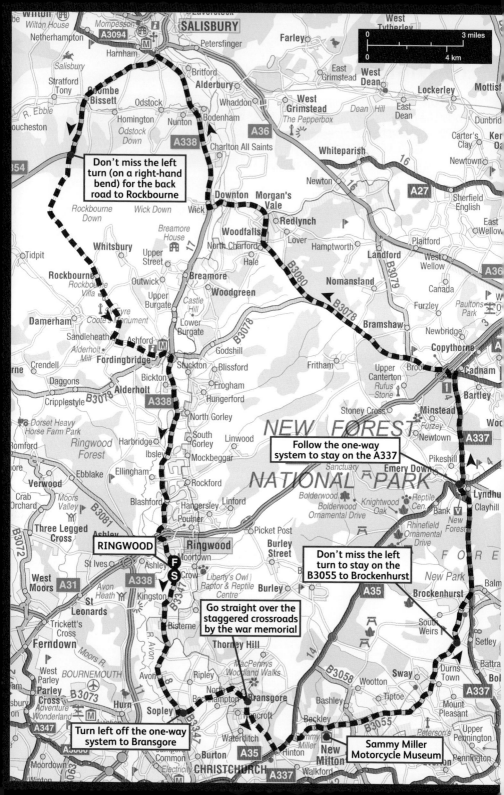

11 Ringwood Cycle

This relaxed ride through the New Forest passes the must-visit Sammy Miller Motorcycle Museum. Watch out for the wild ponies on the open stretches.

FROM	Ringwood
DISTANCE	60 miles
ALLOW	2 hrs

Starting station: Texaco, Christchurch Road, Ringwood BH24 3AN

MILE	LOCATION	TURN	ON	TO	FOR
0	Ringwood	⬑	B3347	**Christchurch**	5
5	Sopley	⬑	minor	**Bransgore**	1.5
6.5	Bransgore	⬏	minor	**Highcliffe**	0.5
7	Bransgore	⬑	minor	**Highcliffe**	2
9	A35 T-junction	⬑	A35	**Lyndhurst**	0.5
9.5	A35	⬏	B3055	**Sway**	7
16.5	B3055	⬑	B3055	**Brockenhurst**	1.5
18	Brockenhurst	⬑ ⬑	A337	**Lyndhurst**	3.5
21.5	Lyndhurst	⬅	A337	**Southampton**	3.5
25	A31/M27 r'bout	↔	B3079	**Brook**	1.5
26.5	Brook	↑	B3078	**Fordingbridge**	3
29.5	Telegraph Hill	↑	B3080	**Downton**	5.5
35	Downton	→	A338	**Salisbury**	5.5
40.5	Salisbury	⬅	A354	**Blandford**	4
44.5	A354	↑	minor	**Rockbourne**	6.5
51	crossroads	⬅	minor	**Fordingbridge**	2
53	Fordingbridge	◆ ⬏	A338	**Ringwood**	7
60	Ringwood				

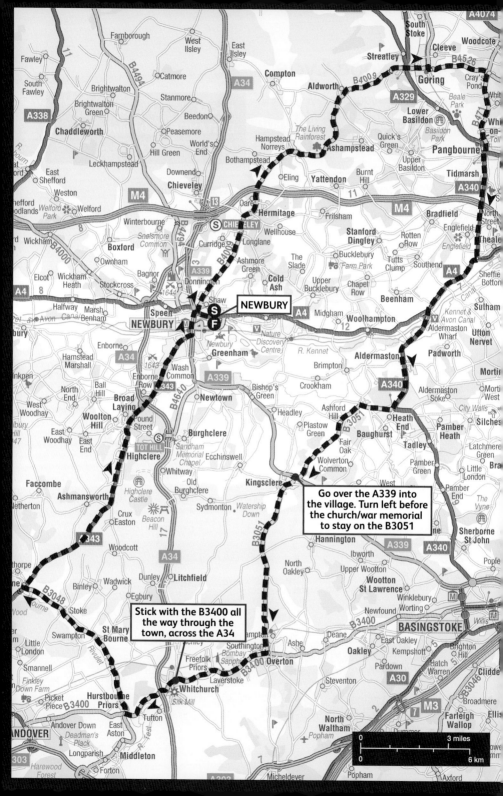

NEWBURY

Go over the A339 into the village. Turn left before the church/war memorial to stay on the B3051

Stick with the B3400 all the way through the town, across the A34

0		3 miles
0		6 km

12 Newbury Rideout

There is some great riding hidden in the low hills of Berkshire. This ride around Newbury aims to avoid the bigger and busier A-roads as much as possible, using the fun B-roads.

FROM	Newbury
DISTANCE	64.5 miles
ALLOW	2 hrs

Starting station: BP, 256 London Road, Newbury RG14 2BS

MILE	LOCATION	TURN	ON	TO	FOR
0	Newbury		B4009	**Hermitage**	7.5
7.5	Hampstead Norreys		B4009	**Aldworth**	7
14.5	Goring		B4526	**Cray's Pond**	2
16.5	Cray's Pond		B471	**Whitchurch**	3
19.5	Pangbourne		A340	**Basingstoke**	3.5
23	A4 roundabout		A4	**Newbury**	3
26	Padworth		A340	**Basingstoke**	3.5
29.5	Aldermaston		B3051	**Kingsclere**	4.5
34	Kingsclere		B3051	**Overton**	6.5
40.5	Overton		B3400	**Salisbury**	5.5
46	Hurstbourne Priors		B3048	**Hurstbourne Tarrant**	6
52	Hurstbourne Tarrant		A343	**Newbury**	12.5
64.5	Newbury				

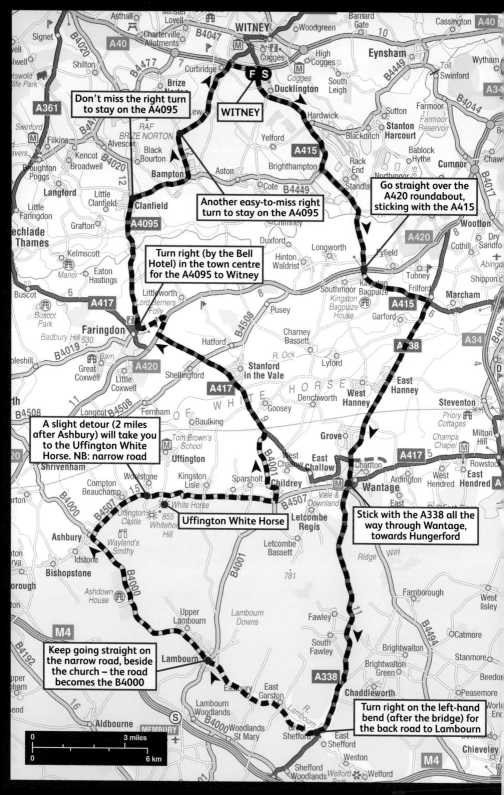

Don't miss the right turn to stay on the A4095

WITNEY

Another easy-to-miss right turn to stay on the A4095

Go straight over the A420 roundabout, sticking with the A415

Turn right (by the Bell Hotel) in the town centre for the A4095 to Witney

A slight detour (2 miles after Ashbury) will take you to the Uffington White Horse. NB: narrow road

Uffington White Horse

Stick with the A338 all the way through Wantage, towards Hungerford

Keep going straight on the narrow road, beside the church – the road becomes the B4000

Turn right on the left-hand bend (after the bridge) for the back road to Lambourn

0   3 miles
0   6 km

13 Witney and the White Horse

There's a little functional riding on this route, heading south to Wantage, to get on the best roads, looping out past the Uffington White Horse and back through Bampton (made famous by Downton Abbey).

FROM	Witney
DISTANCE	64 miles
ALLOW	1 hr 50 mins

Starting station: Shell, Ducklington Lane, Witney OX28 4TT

MILE	LOCATION	TURN	ON	TO	FOR
0	Witney	⊙↱	A415	**Abingdon**	10.5
10.5	Frilford	🚦↱	A338	**Wantage**	5.5
16	Wantage	⊙	A338	**Wantage**	1
17	Wantage	↱ 🚦	A338	**Hungerford**	8.5
25.5	Great Shefford	↱	minor	**East Garston**	11
36.5	Ashbury	↱	B4507	**Kingston Lisle**	6.5
43	B4507 crossroads	┿	B4001	**Challow Station**	2.5
45.5	A417 T-junction	↰	A417	**Faringdon**	5
50.5	A420 roundabout	⊙↱	A420	**Oxford**	0.5
51	A420	↰	minor	**Faringdon**	1
52	Faringdon	↱	A4095	**Witney**	4
56	Clanfield	↱	A4095	**Witney**	3.5
59.5	A4095	↱	A4095	**Witney**	4.5
64	Witney				

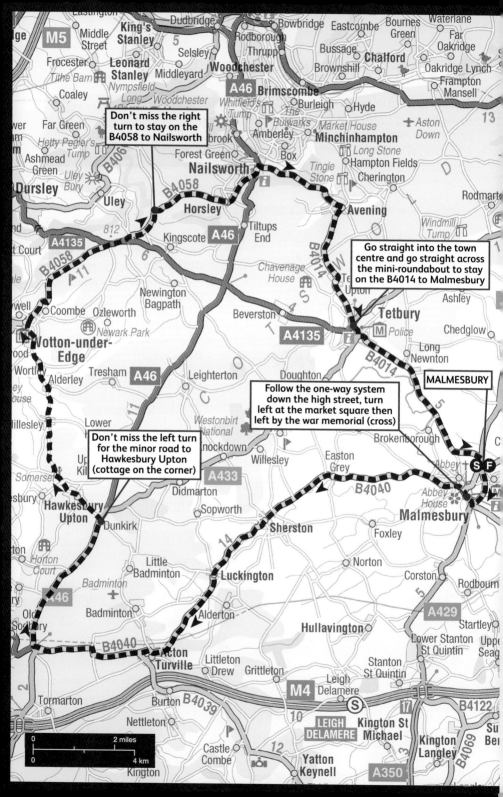

14 Malmesbury Miles

This is another run through the Cotswolds. My favourite road is the one from the A46 to Wotton-under-Edge which I first found by accident – proving there's no sugh thing as a wrong turn, just alternative directions…

FROM	Malmesbury
DISTANCE	43 miles
ALLOW	1 hr 15 mins

Starting station: BP, Crudwell Road, Malmesbury SN16 9JL

MILE	LOCATION	TURN	ON	TO	FOR
0	Malmesbury	⟳	A429	**Chippenham (M4)**	1
1	Priory roundabout	⟳→ ↰	B4040	**Town centre**	10.5
11.5	Acton Turville	↰ ↱	B4040	**Yate**	3
14.5	A46 T-junction	↱	A46	**Stroud**	4
18.5	A46	↰	minor	**Hawkesbury Upton**	5.5
24	Wotton-under-Edge	⟳→	B4058	**Nailsworth**	3
27	A4135 T-junction	↱ ↰	B4058	**Stroud**	1.5
28.5	B4058	↱	B4058	**Nailsworth**	3
31.5	Nailsworth	↰ ↱	B4014	**Avening**	6.5
38	Tetbury	↑ ⟳	B4014	**Malmesbury**	5
43	Malmesbury				

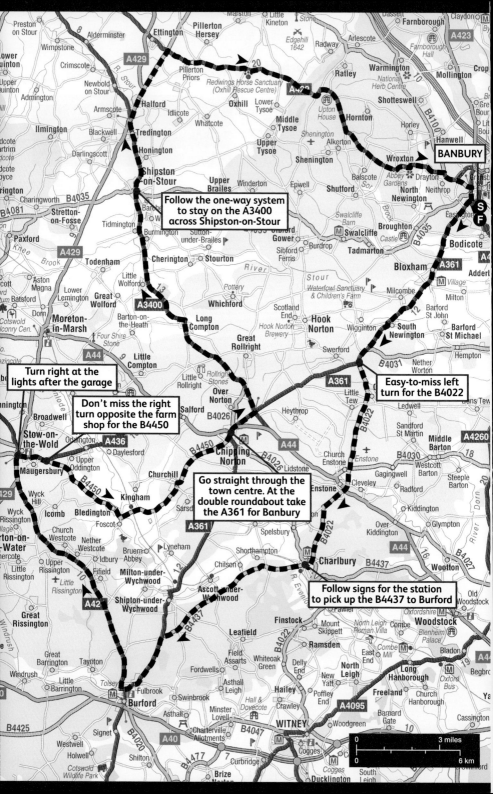

Follow the one-way system to stay on the A3400 across Shipston-on-Stour

Turn right at the lights after the garage

Don't miss the right turn opposite the farm shop for the B4450

Easy-to-miss left turn for the B4022

Go straight through the town centre. At the double roundabout take the A361 for Banbury

Follow signs for the station to pick up the B4437 to Burford

BANBURY

15 Banbury Rideout

I must thank the nicest man in motorcycling, Dan Sagar, for helping refine this route through his Cotswold stomping ground. It's packed with classic biking roads – and one or two surprises.

FROM	Banbury
DISTANCE	74.5 miles
ALLOW	2 hrs

Starting station: Sainsbury's, Oxford Road, Banbury OX16 9XA

MILE	LOCATION	TURN	ON	TO	FOR
0	Banbury		A361	**Chipping Norton**	7.5
7.5	A361		B4022	**Enstone**	4
11.5	B4030 junction		B4022	**Enstone**	1
12.5	A44 junction		B4022	**Charlbury**	3.5
16	Charlbury		B4437	**Burford**	6
22	A361 junction		A361	**Burford**	2.5
24.5	Burford		A424	**Stow**	9
33.5	A429 junction		A429	**Stow**	0.5
34	Stow-on-the-Wold		A436	**Chipping Norton**	1
35	A436		B4450	**Bledington**	9
44	Chipping Norton		A44	**Town centre**	400 m
44	Chipping Norton		A3400	**Long Compton**	13.5
57.5	Fosse Way		A429	**Halford**	1
58.5	Halford		B4455	**Leicester**	2
60.5	A422 T-junction		A422	**Banbury**	14
74.5	Banbury				

England – East and Southeast

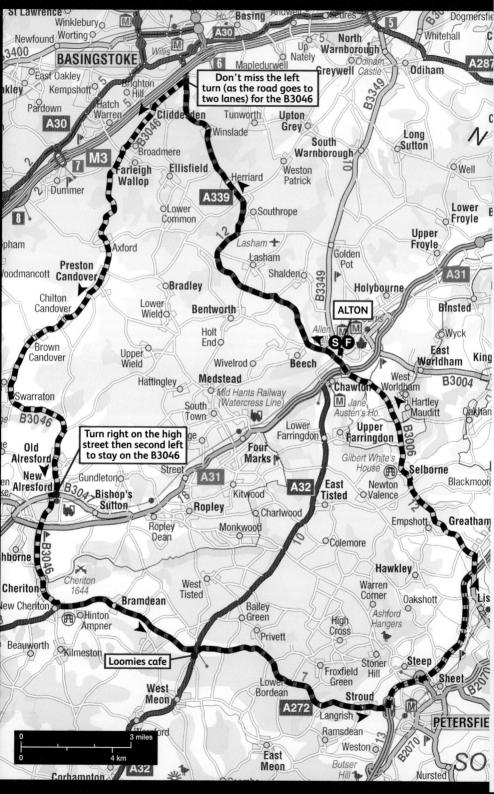

16 Alton Powers

I don't normally use dual carriageways, but this route uses a short stretch of the A3 to avoid a lot of suburban slog through Petersfield. For the rest, it's classic biking roads – heading out to popular biking cafe Loomies.

FROM	Alton
DISTANCE	52 miles
ALLOW	1 hr 30 mins

Starting station: BP, 5 Butts Road, Alton GU34 1LH

MILE	LOCATION	TURN	ON	TO	FOR
0	Alton	↰ ⟳ ↱	A339	**Basingstoke**	11
11	Basingstoke	↰	B3046	**Cliddesden**	14.5
25.5	New Alresford	↱ ↰	B3046	**Cheriton**	3.5
29	Cheriton	↰	A272	**Bramdean**	10.5
39.5	Petersfield	←⟳	A3	**London**	3.5
43	Ham Barn r'bout	←⟳	B3006	**Selborne**	9
52	Alton				

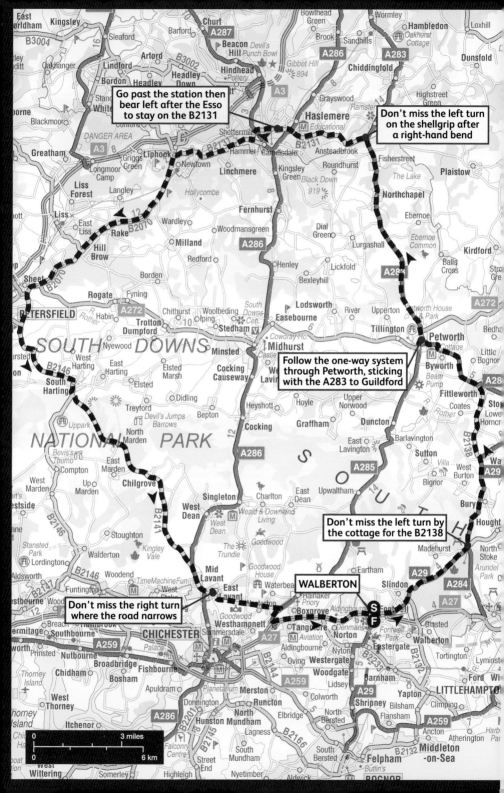

17 Arundel Trundle

This route passes close to Goodwood, the cradle of British motorsport. I don't recommend racing round this route, though: enjoy the gentle flow on these lovely roads.

FROM	Walberton, Arundel
DISTANCE	56 miles
ALLOW	1 hr 30 min

Starting station: Shell, Arundel Road, Walberton, Arundel BN18 0SB

MILE	LOCATION	TURN	ON	TO	FOR
0	Walberton		A27	**Worthing**	0.5
0.5	A29 roundabout		A29	**Slindon**	4
4.5	Whiteways Lodge		A29	**Pulborough**	3
7.5	Watersfield		B2138	**Fittleworth**	3
10.5	Fittleworth		A283	**Petworth**	10
20.5	A238		B2131	**Haslemere**	4
24.5	Haslemere		B2131	**Liphook**	3.5
28	Liphook		B2070	**Rake**	7
35	Petersfield		B2199	**South Harting**	1
36	Petersfield		B2146	**South Harting**	4
40	South Harting		B2141	**Chichester**	8
48	A286 junction		A286	**Chichester**	1
49	Lavant		minor	**East Lavant**	0.5
49.5	East Lavant		minor	**Goodwood**	2.5
52	A258 junction		A258	**Chichester**	0.5
52.5	A27 roundabout		A27	**Worthing**	3.5
56	Walberton				

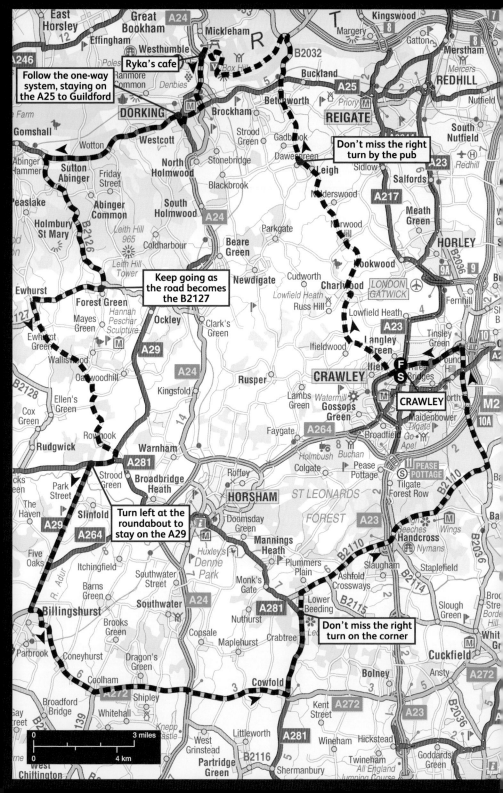

18 Box Hill Blast

Ryka's at Box Hill is a must-visit – not just because it's a popular bike cafe with some handy nearby hairpins, but also because it's all the excuse you need to ride this route!

FROM	Crawley
DISTANCE	67.5 miles
ALLOW	2 hr 10 mins

Starting station: Sainsbury's, Crawley Avenue, Crawley RH10 8NF

MILE	LOCATION	TURN	ON	TO	FOR
0	Crawley		minor	**Langley Green**	3.5
3.5	Charlwood		minor	**Leigh**	5
8.5	Leigh		minor	**no signpost**	2.5
11	Betchworth		B2032	**Tadworth**	1.5
12.5	Betchworth		minor	**Box Hill**	4
16.5	B2209 junction		A24	**Dorking**	1.5
18	Deepdene r'bout		A25	**Dorking**	6
24	Abinger Hammer		B2126	**Holmbury St Mary**	7
31	Ewhurst		B2127	**Cranleigh**	0.5
31.5	Ewhurst		minor	**Ellen's Green**	5
36.5	A29 T-junction		A29	**Bognor Regis**	1.5
38	Clemsfold		A29	**Bognor Regis**	4
42	Billingshurst		A272	**Coneyhurst**	9.5
51.5	Cowfold		A281	**Horsham**	2.5
54	Lower Beeding		B2110	**Gatwick**	4
58	Handcross		B2110	**Turners Hill**	3.5
61.5	B2036 T-junction		B2036	**Horley**	6
67.5	Crawley				

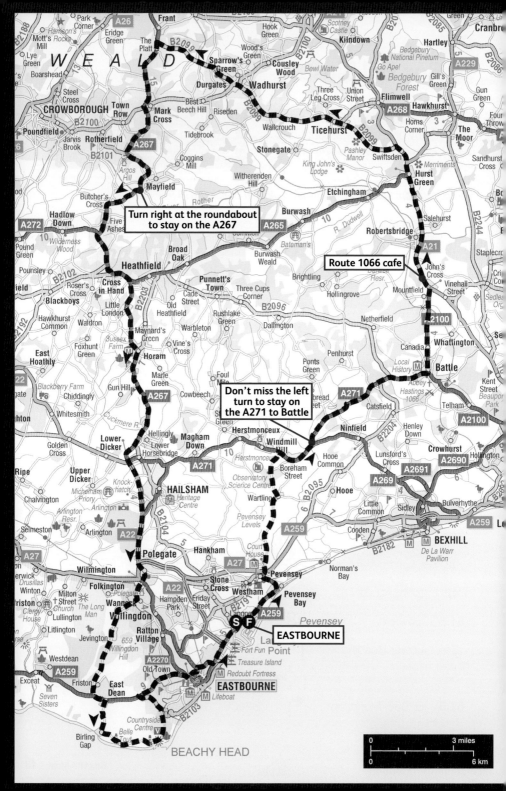

19 South Coast Classic

While this route finishes with the run from Birling Gap to Beachy Head, the heart of it is further inland, linking flowing roads together while trying to dodge the traffic.

FROM	Eastbourne
DISTANCE	71 miles
ALLOW	2 hrs

Starting station: Asda, The Crumbles, Pevensey Bay Road, Eastbourne BN23 6JH

MILE	LOCATION	TURN	ON	TO	FOR
0	Eastbourne		A259	**Hastings**	3
3	A27 roundabout		minor	**Wartling**	4.5
7.5	A271 junction		A271	**Battle**	7
14.5	Battle		A2100	**Sevenoaks**	3
17.5	John's Cross		A21	**London**	4
21.5	Hurst Green		B2099	**Ticehurst**	10.5
32	A267 juntion		A267	**Mark Cross**	18
50	Boship r'bout		A22	**Hailsham**	4
54	A27 roundabout		B2247	**Polegate**	0.5
54.5	Polegate		minor	**Town centre**	5
59.5	Friston		A259	**Eastbourne**	0.5
60	Friston		minor	**Birling Gap**	6
66	A259 junction		A259	**Town centre**	5
71	Eastbourne				

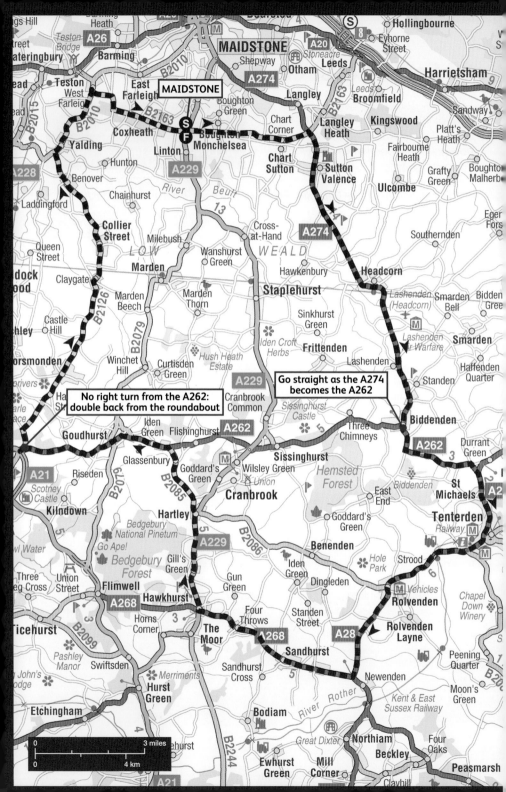

20 Maidstone Cold Brilliant

The garden of England hides some lovely riding – all those roads that have grown up over the years can blossom into a fabulous ride, if you let them – just like this!

FROM	Maidstone
DISTANCE	51 miles
ALLOW	1 hr 30 mins

Starting station: Shell, Linton Road, Loose, Maidstone ME15 0AT

MILE	LOCATION	TURN	ON	TO	FOR
0	Maidstone	↱ ⬅🚦	B2163	**Leeds**	3.5
3.5	Sutton Valence	↱	A274	**Tenterden**	12
15.5	A28 junction	↱	A28	**Tenterden**	7.5
23	A268 junction	↱	A268	**Hawkhurst**	5
28	Hawkhurst	🚦↱	A229	**Cranbrook**	2.5
30.5	Hartley	↰	B2085	**Goudhurst (A262)**	2
32.5	A262 junction	↰	A262	**Tunbridge Wells**	4.5
37	roundabout	↻	B2162	**Horsmonden**	9
46	Yalding	↱	B2010	**Wateringbury**	2
48	West Farleigh	↱	B2163	**Coxheath**	3
51	Maidstone				

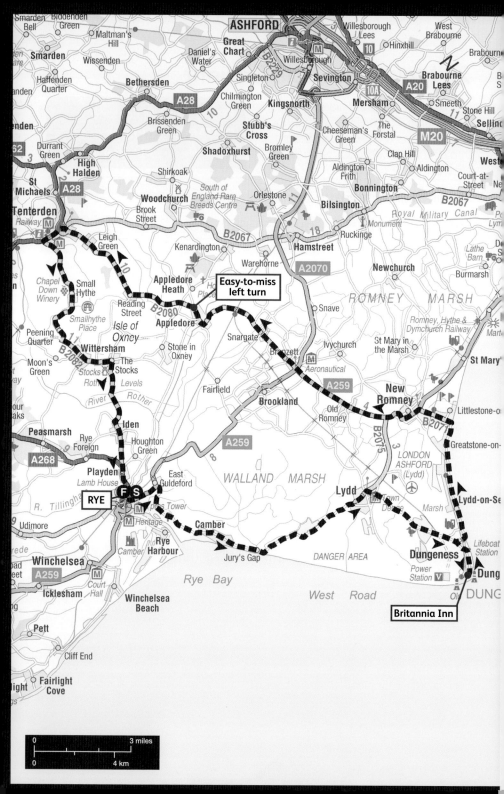

21 Rye's Miles

I love the wilder, windswept corners of the South Coast, but after looping out past Romney Marsh, this route heads inland on roads that are sure to make you grin.

FROM	Rye
DISTANCE	45.5 miles
ALLOW	1 hr 15 mins

Starting station: Murco, 74 Fishmarket Road, Rye TN31 7LP

MILE	LOCATION	TURN	ON	TO	FOR
0	Rye	↱ ↔⭕	A259	**Folkestone**	1
1	East Guldeford	↱	minor	**Camber**	9
10	Lydd	⭕→	minor	**Dungeness**	3
13	Dungeness	↱	minor	**Old Lighthouse**	2.5*

* This is a dead-end road. Enjoy the view then ride back

MILE	LOCATION	TURN	ON	TO	FOR
15.5	Dungeness	↱	minor	**Littlestone**	3.5
19	Littlestone	↰	B2071	**New Romney**	1
20	New Romney	↰	A259	**Hastings**	4.5
24.5	Brenzett	⭕	B2080	**Tenterden**	4.5
29	Appledore	↰	B2080	**Tenterden**	5
34	Tenterden	↰↰	A28	**Town centre**	0.5
34.5	Tenterden	⬅🚦	B2082	**Rye**	11
45.5	Rye				

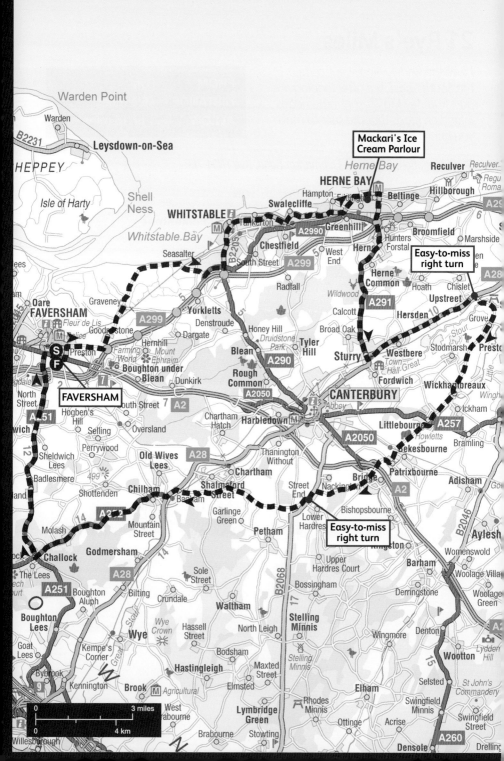

22 Don't Miss Faversham

Kent can be a congested county and this route does cut through suburbia as it runs out to Herne Bay, before breaking free of the traffic to romp through the countryside.

FROM	Faversham
DISTANCE	50 miles
ALLOW	1 hr 40 mins

Starting station: Shell, Canterbury Road, Faversham ME13 8XA

MILE	LOCATION	TURN	ON	TO	FOR
0	Faversham	↰↱	B2040	**Graveney**	0.5
0.5	Faversham	⟲→	minor	**Graveney**	1
1.5	crossroads	↰	minor	**Goodnestone**	6
7.5	Whitstable	↱←⟲	A2990	**Margate**	2.5
10	Whitstable	←⟲⟲→	B2205	**Herne Bay**	3
13	Herne Bay	←⟲↱	minor	**Sea front**	1
14	Herne Bay	↑	B2205	**Canterbury**	1
15	A299 junction	⟲→←⟲	A291	**Canterbury**	5
20	Sturry	↰	A28	**Margate**	4
24	Upstreet	↱	minor	**Grove Ferry**	5
29	Littlebourne	↥	minor	**Bekesbourne**	2
31	Patrixbourne	⟲→	minor	**Canterbury**	1
32	crossroads	↑	minor	**Pett Bottom**	2
34	B2068 T-junction	↰	B2068	**Lower Hardres**	0.5
34.5	B2068	↱	minor	**Chartham**	4.5
39	A28 T-junction	↰	A28	**Ashford**	4.5
43.5	Challock	⟲→	A251	**Faversham**	6.5
50	Faversham				

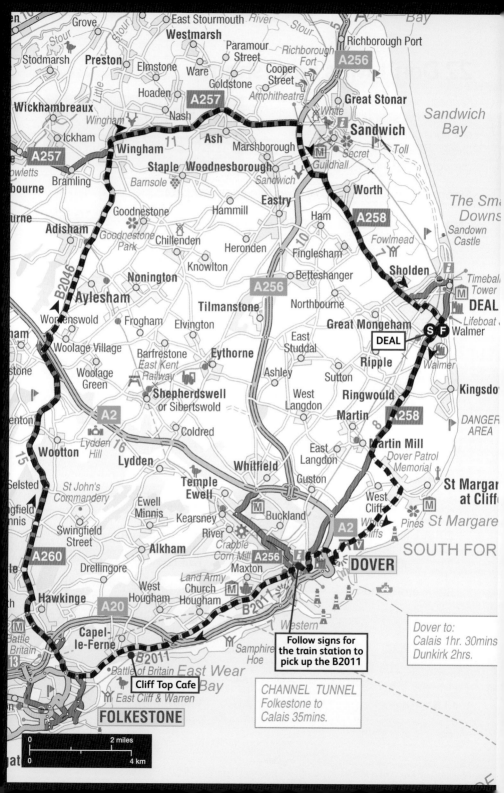

23 Big Deal

There's much more to Dover than the white cliffs and the port – there's plenty of great riding away from the main roads, as this loop from Deal reveals.

FROM	Deal
DISTANCE	41 miles
ALLOW	1 hr 20 mins

Starting station: Esso, Dover Road, Walmer, Deal CT14 7JH

MILE	LOCATION	TURN	ON	TO	FOR
0	Deal	↱	A258	**Dover**	3.5
3.5	A258	↰	minor	**St Margaret's at Cliffe**	1
4.5	St Margaret's at Cliffe	↱	minor	**White Cliffs**	3.5
8	Dover	◀🚦	A258	**Dover**	0.5
8.5	Dover	🚦▶ 🚦▶	A256	⇌	0.5
9	Dover	◀○	B2011	**Maxton**	6.5
15.5	Folkestone	○ ○▶	A260	**Hawkinge**	9
24.5	A2 junction	○▶ ○	B2046	**Aylesham**	5
29.5	Wingham	↑	A257	**Sandwich**	5
34.5	Sandwich	○▶	A256	**Dover**	1
35.5	Sandwich	◀○ ○▶	A258	**Deal**	5.5
41	Deal				

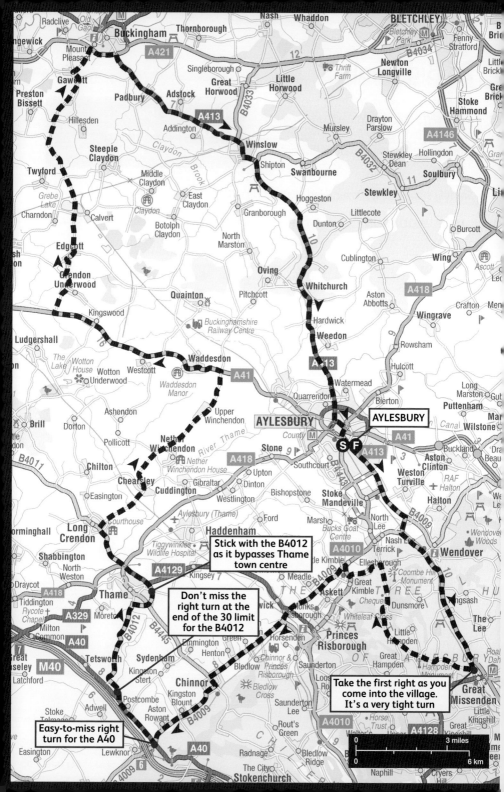

Stick with the B4012 as it bypasses Thame town centre

Don't miss the right turn at the end of the 30 limit for the B4012

Take the first right as you come into the village. It's a very tight turn

Easy-to-miss right turn for the A40

24 Aylesbury Loop

I got some help on this route from Andy Rouse, the YouTube star known as The Missenden Flyer. You might recognize some of the roads in his videos – check out his channel to see if you can spot them.

FROM	Aylesbury
DISTANCE	74 miles
ALLOW	2 hrs 15 mins

Starting station: Esso, Wendover Road, Aylesbury HP21 9LB

MILE	LOCATION	TURN	ON	TO	FOR
0	Aylesbury	↰	A413	**Amersham**	8.5
8.5	A413	↱	minor	**Great Missenden**	0.5
9	Great Missenden	↱	minor	**Butler's Cross**	5.5
14.5	Butler's Cross	↰	minor	**Lt & Gt Kimble**	1
15.5	Little Kimble	↱	A4010	**Aylesbury**	0.5
16	Little Kimble	↰	B4009	**Chinnor**	6
22	Chinnor	↰ ⟳↱	B4009	**Lewknor**	3
25	B4009	↱	A40	**Oxford**	1.5
26.5	A40	↱	B4012	**Thame**	5.5
32	Thame	⟳↱ ⟳↑	B4011	**Long Crendon**	2
34	Long Crendon	⟳↱	minor	**Chearsley**	1.5
35.5	Chearsley	↑	minor	**Waddesdon**	5
40.5	Waddesdon	↰	A41	**Bicester**	6
46.5	A41	↱	minor	**Calvert**	8.5
55	Gawcott	↱	minor	**Buckingham**	1
56	Buckingham	⟳↱ ⟳↱	A413	**Aylesbury**	18
74	Aylesbury				

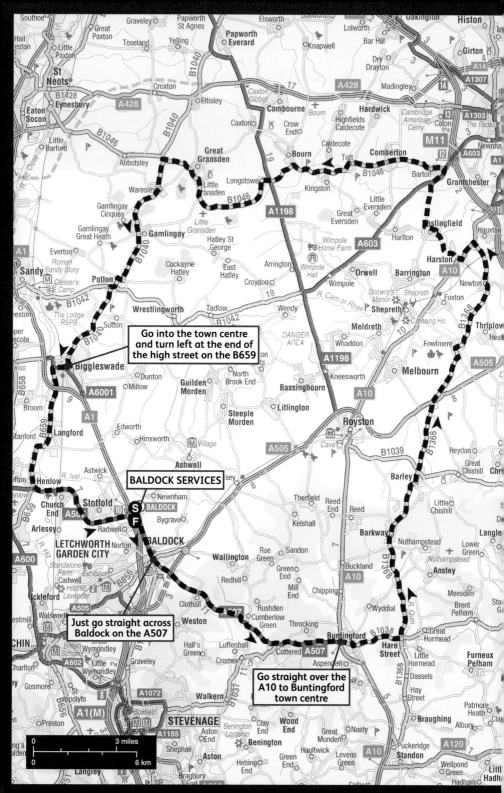

Go into the town centre and turn left at the end of the high street on the B659

BALDOCK SERVICES

Just go straight across Baldock on the A507

Go straight over the A10 to Buntingford town centre

25 Dandy, Fine and Baldock

The basis for this route was an accidental ride: filling up at Baldock Services, I couldn't face getting back on the A1(M). What I found instead were a load of good-fun roads. Much better!

FROM	Baldock
DISTANCE	**65 miles**
ALLOW	**2 hrs**

Starting station: Baldock Services, A1(M) J10, Radwell, Baldock SG7 5TR

MILE	LOCATION	TURN	ON	TO	FOR
0	Baldock Services	⟳	A507	**Baldock**	6
6	T-junction	↱	A507	**Buntingford**	4.5
10.5	Buntingford	↱ ↰	B1038	**Hare Street**	2
12.5	Hare Street	↰	B1368	**Barley**	8.5
21	Flint Cross	↱ ↑	B1368	**Fowlmere**	6.5
27.5	Harston	◀🚦	A10	**Royston**	1
28.5	Harston	↱	minor	**Haslingfield**	4
32.5	A603 T-junction	↱	A603	**Cambridge**	0.5
33	Barton	↰	B1046	**Comberton**	7
40	A1198	↥	B1046	**Gransdens**	6
46	B1040 T-junction	↰	B1040	**Biggleswade**	9
55	Biggleswade	↱◀⟳	B659	**Langford**	5
60	Henlow	◀⟳	A507	**Baldock**	5
65	Baldock Services				

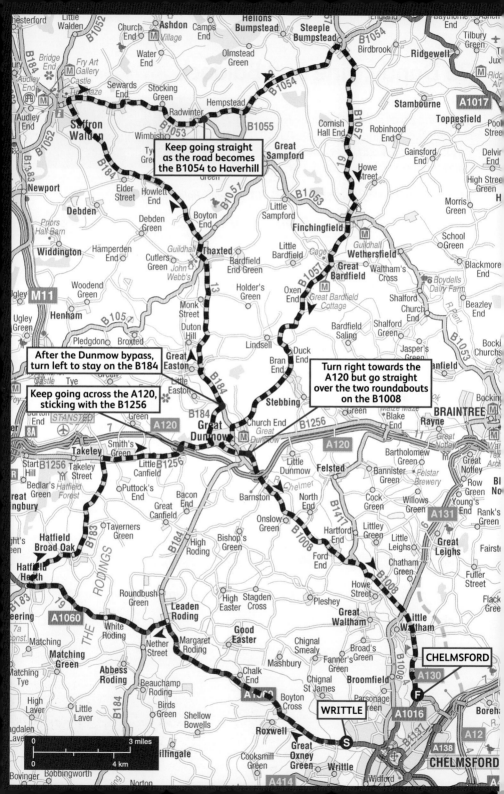

Keep going straight as the road becomes the B1054 to Haverhill

After the Dunmow bypass, turn left to stay on the B184

Keep going across the A120, sticking with the B1256

Turn right towards the A120 but go straight over the two roundabouts on the B1008

CHELMSFORD

WRITTLE

26 The Only Way in Essex

While this route from the edge of Chelmsford is built around the famous B1057, the joy of it is that it brings in so many other great biking roads, making it a two-hour grin-fest.

FROM	Writtle, Chelmsford
DISTANCE	73 miles
ALLOW	2 hrs

Starting station: BP, Roxwell Road, Writtle, Chelmsford CM1 3RU

MILE	LOCATION	TURN	ON	TO	FOR
0	Writtle	↰	A1060	**The Rodings**	12
12	Hatfield Heath	↱	B183	**Hatfield Broad Oak**	5.5
17.5	Takeley	🚦↱	B1256	**Great Dunmow**	3.5
21	Woodlands	↺	B184	**Thaxted**	13.5
34.5	Saffron Walden	🚦↱	B1053	**Finchingfield**	10
44.5	Steeple Bumpstead	↱	B1057	**Finchingfield**	5.5
50	T-junction	↱	B1057	**Finchingfield**	0.5
50.5	Finchingfield	↱	B1057	**Great Bardfield**	8.5
59	Great Dunmow	↰	minor	**Town centre**	1.5
60.5	Great Dunmow	↱ 🚦	B1008	**Felsted**	6.5
67	roundabout	↺	A130	**Chelmsford**	6
73	Chelmsford				

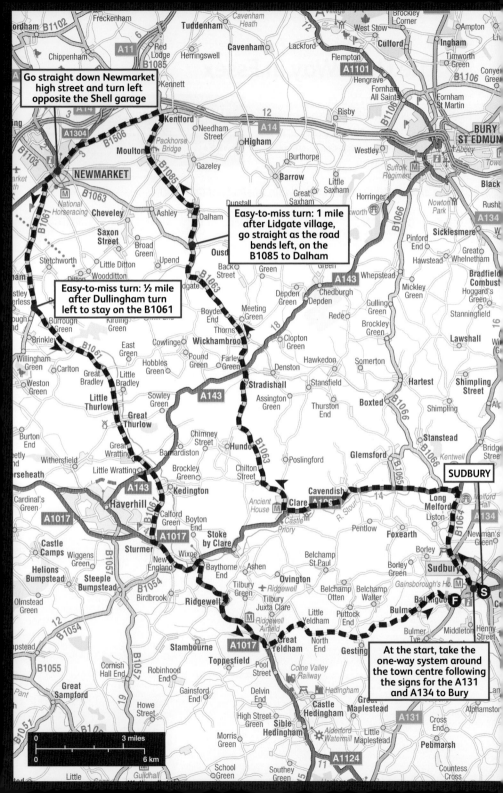

Go straight down Newmarket high street and turn left opposite the Shell garage

Easy-to-miss turn: 1 mile after Lidgate village, go straight as the road bends left, on the B1085 to Dalham

Easy-to-miss turn: ½ mile after Dullingham turn left to stay on the B1061

At the start, take the one-way system around the town centre following the signs for the A131 and A134 to Bury

27 Sudbury Rideout

This is one of my regular, favourite weekend rides, especially handy after a trip to the Adventure Bike Shop in Sudbury. Just watch out for horses in Newmarket.

FROM	Sudbury
DISTANCE	61 miles
ALLOW	2 hrs

Starting station: BP, Cornard Road, Sudbury CO10 2XA

MILE	LOCATION	TURN	ON	TO	FOR
0	Sudbury		A134	**Bury St Edmunds**	2
2	Sudbury		B1064	**Long Melford**	2
4	Long Melford		A1092	**Clare**	6.5
10.5	Clare		B1063	**Newmarket**	5.5
16	A143 junction		B1063	**Newmarket**	5
21	B1063		B1085	**Dalham**	5.5
26.5	Kentford		B1506	**Newmarket**	3
29.5	Newmarket		A1304	**Newmarket**	1.5
31	Newmarket		B1061	**Haverhill**	4.5
35.5	B1061		B1061	**Haverhill**	7.5
43	A143 junction		B1061	**Haverhill**	2
45	Sturmer		A1017	**Braintree**	7
52	Great Yeldham		minor	**Little Yeldham**	9
61	Sudbury				

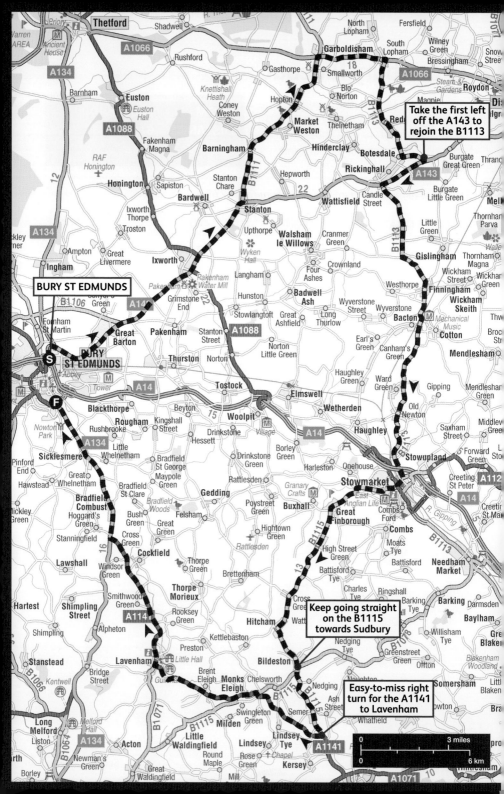

28 Juicy Bury

I grew up riding the roads around here and, more than 30 years later, I still enjoy them. This route loops out to the half-timbered village of Lavenham – a great place.

FROM	**Bury St Edmunds**
DISTANCE	**66 miles**
ALLOW	**1 hr 45 mins**

Starting station: Tesco, St Saviours Interchange, Bury St Edmunds IP32 7JS

MILE	LOCATION	TURN	ON	TO	FOR
0	Bury St Edmunds	○↑	A143	**Diss**	9.5
9.5	Stanton	↰	B1111	**Garboldisham**	6
15.5	Garboldisham	↱	A1066	**Diss**	2.5
18	South Lopham	↱	B1113	**Botesdale**	4.5
22.5	Botesdale	↱	A143	**Bury St Edmunds**	1.5
24	A143	↰	B1113	**Stowmarket**	11
35	Stowmarket	○→	B1115	**Sudbury**	12
47	B1115	↱	A1141	**Lavenham**	7
54	Lavenham	↱	A1141	**Bury St Edmunds**	5
59	A134 junction	↱	A134	**Bury St Edmunds**	7
66	Bury St Edmunds				

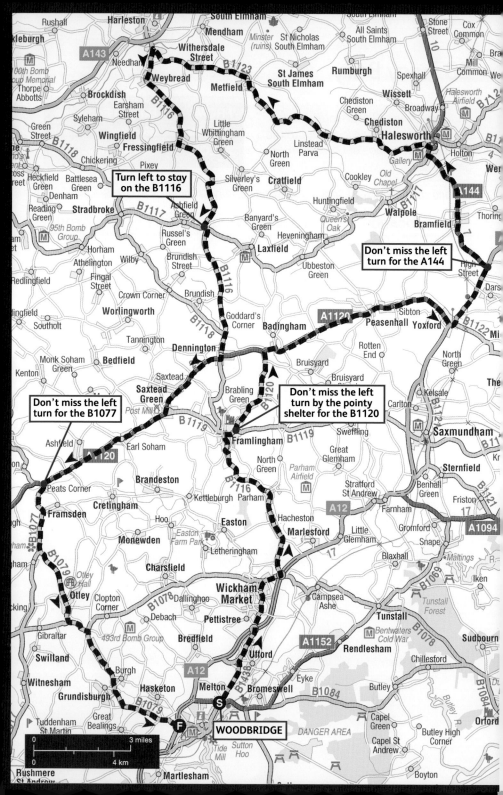

Turn left to stay on the B1116

Don't miss the left turn for the A144

Don't miss the left turn by the pointy shelter for the B1120

Don't miss the left turn for the B1077

WOODBRIDGE

29 Suffolk Punch

This is a route I've been refining for a while – which improved no end when I stopped trying to force it out to the coast. Instead it just uses quiet, flowing, great-riding roads.

FROM	Woodbridge
DISTANCE	66.5 miles
ALLOW	2 hrs

Starting station: Gulf, Melton Road, Melton, Woodbridge IP12 1NT

MILE	LOCATION	TURN	ON	TO	FOR
0	Woodbridge	←	B1438	**Ufford**	2
2	T-junction	→	B1438	**Ufford**	3
5	A12 roundabout	⟷	B1116	**Framlingham**	5
10	Framlingham	→←	B1120	**Badingham**	3.5
13.5	A1120 junction	→	A1120	**Yoxford**	6.5
20	Yoxford	←	A12	**Lowestoft**	2
22	A12	←	A144	**Halesworth**	4
26	Halesworth	→←	B1123	**Harleston**	11
37	B1116 junction	←	B1116	**Fressingfield**	11
48	Dennington	→	A1120	**Stowmarket**	7
55	A1120	←	B1077	**Ipswich**	2.5
57.5	Helmingham Hall	←	B1079	**Woodbridge**	9
66.5	Woodbridge				

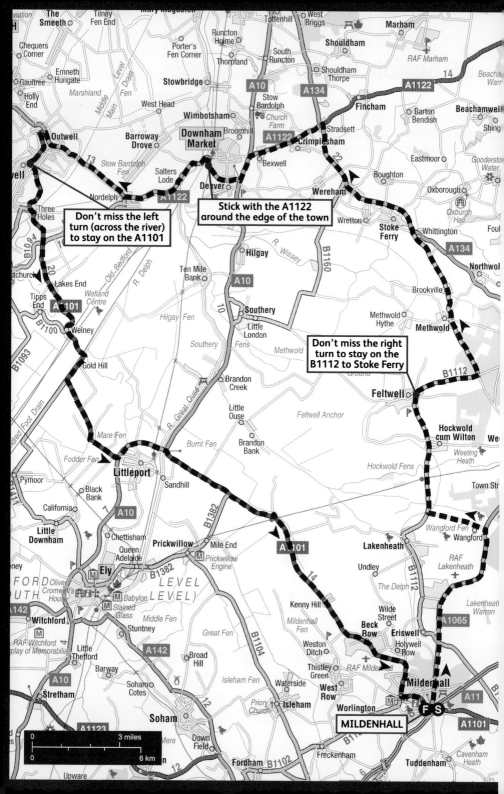

30 Mildenhall Miles

*The Fens aren't big on hills, but they have
their own challenges – rumpled surfaces,
tight corners. Here's a fun run that's
handy for the popular Walkers tea stop.*

FROM	Mildenhall
DISTANCE	67.5 miles
ALLOW	1 hr 45 mins

Starting station: Shell, 5 Fiveways Roundabout, Barton Mills, Mildenhall IP28 6AE

MILE	LOCATION	TURN	ON	TO	FOR
0	Mildenhall	↰	A1065	**Brandon**	7
7	airfield	⬅🚦	minor	**Lakenheath**	2
9	T-junction	↱	B1112	**Hockwold**	4
13	Feltwell	↱	B1112	**Stoke Ferry**	2
15	T-junction	↰	B1112	**Stoke Ferry**	5.5
20.5	roundabout	⬆	A134	**King's Lynn**	5.5
26	Stradsett	↰	A1122	**Downham Market**	2.5
28.5	roundabout	⬅	A10	**Ely**	1
29.5	roundabout	➡	A1122	**Wisbech**	9
38.5	Outwell	⬅	A1101	**Upwell**	0.5
39	Upwell	↰	A1101	**Littleport**	12.5
51.5	Littleport	⬅	A10	**Downham Market**	2
53.5	Littleport	⬆	A1101	**Mildenhall**	14
67.5	Mildenhall				

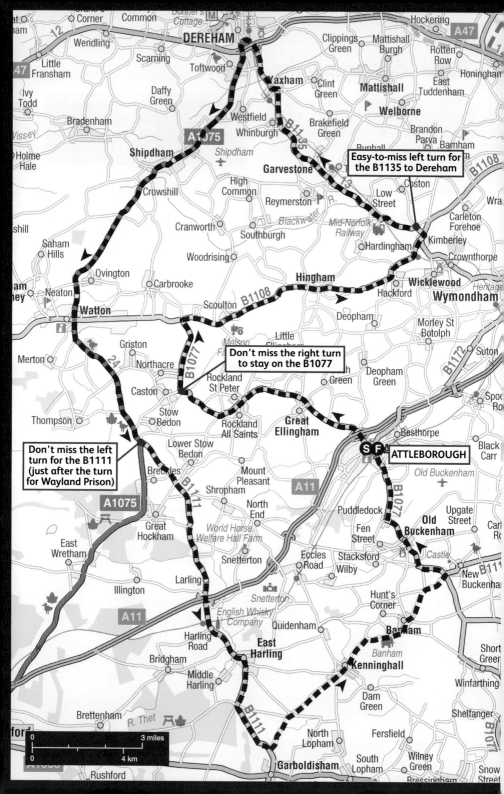

31 Brecks Where I Belong

*Norfolk's Breckland isn't a big area,
but I have a soft spot for it – it's where
I live, after all. This route comes from
meeting my pal Ian for a quick ride
around Attleborough.*

FROM	Attleborough
DISTANCE	58.5 miles
ALLOW	1 hr 40 mins

Starting station: Sainsbury's, High Street, Attleborough NR17 2EH

MILE	LOCATION	TURN	ON	TO	FOR
0	Attleborough	↰ ↰	B1077	**Watton**	6.5
6.5	B1077	↱	B1077	**Watton**	2
8.5	B1108 crossroad	↱	B1108	**Norwich**	7.5
16	Kimberley	↰	B1135	**Dereham**	8
24	Dereham	◁🚦	A1075	**Watton**	13
37	A1075	↑	B1111	**East Harling**	10
47	Garboldisham	↰	minor	**Kenninghall**	7
54	Dam Brigg crossroads	↰	B1077	**Attleborough**	4.5
58.5	Attleborough				

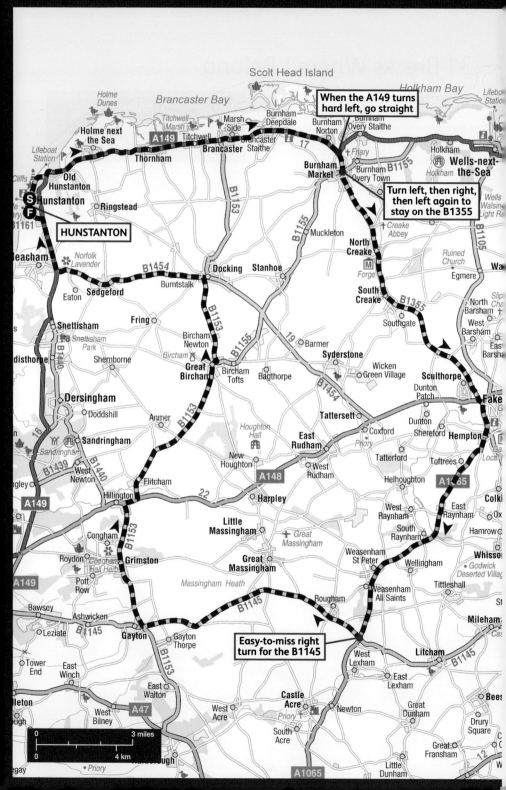

When the A149 turns hard left, go straight

Turn left, then right, then left again to stay on the B1355

Easy-to-miss right turn for the B1145

HUNSTANTON

32 Hunstanton Deliver

I live quite near Sunny Hunny so I've been tinkering with this route each time I ride it to get it just right. This version does use a stretch of the often-busy A149 coast road, but after that it's quiet, flowing roads all the way.

FROM	Hunstanton
DISTANCE	58.5 miles
ALLOW	1 hr 30 mins

Starting station: Tesco, Southend Road, Hunstanton PE36 5AR

MILE	LOCATION	TURN	ON	TO	FOR
0	Hunstanton	↱	B1161	**Town centre**	1.5
1.5	A149 junction	↰	A149	**Brancaster**	10.5
12	A149	↰	B1355	**Fakenham**	9
21	A148	↰	A148	**Cromer**	0.5
21.5	roundabout	⟳→	A1065	**Swaffham**	9
30.5	A1065	↱	B1145	**King's Lynn**	8
38.5	Gayton	↱	B1153	**Grimston**	4.5
43	Hillington	↱↰	B1153	**Flitcham**	8
51	Docking	↰	B1454	**Heacham**	5.5
56.5	Heacham	🚦→	A149	**Hunstanton**	2
58.5	Hunstanton				

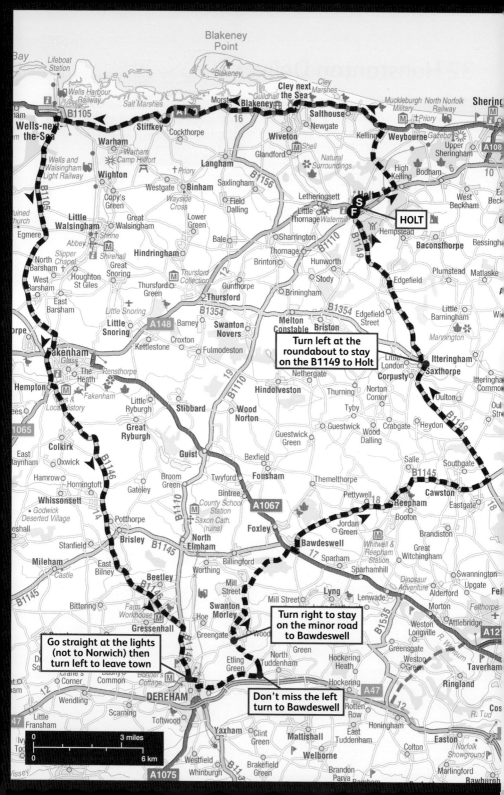

33 Holt on to Your Hat

The North Norfolk coast is beautiful – but be warned: it is also busy. That's why, after admiring its most scenic stretch, this route loops inland for brilliant, quiet roads.

FROM	Holt
DISTANCE	66 miles
ALLOW	1 hr 50 mins

Starting station: BP, 33–35 Cromer Road, Holt NR25 6EU

MILE	LOCATION	TURN	ON	TO	FOR
0	Holt	↰	minor	**Cromer**	1
1	A148 junction	↰	A148	**Cromer**	0.5
1.5	A148	↰	minor	**Holt RFC**	2.5
4	Kelling	↰	A149	**Hunstanton**	12.5
16.5	Wells-next-the-Sea	↰	B1105	**Fakenham**	8
24.5	T-junction	↱	B1105	**Fakenham**	0.5
25	A148	↱⟳	A1065	**Swaffham**	1
26	Hempton	↰	B1146	**Dereham**	6
32	B1145	↱	B1146	**Dereham**	4
36	T-junction	↱	B1146	**Dereham**	2
38	Dereham	↑ ⟳	minor	**Through traffic**	300 m
38	Dereham	🚦↰	minor	**no sign**	1.5
39.5	Dereham	↰	minor	**Swanton Morley**	1
40.5	minor road	↰	minor	**Bawdeswell**	7
47.5	A1067	↱↰	B1145	**Reepham**	4
51.5	Reepham	↰	B1145	**B1145**	4
55.5	roundabout	↔⟳	B1149	**Holt**	10.5
66	Holt				

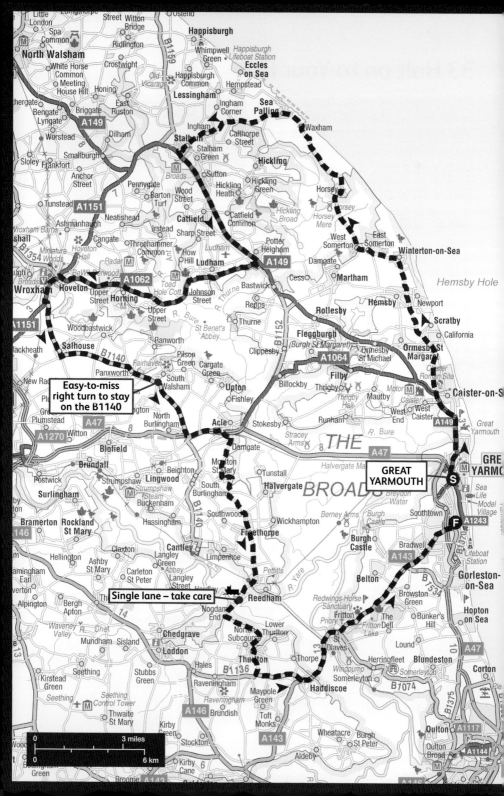

34 Broads and More

I always loved going to Great Yarmouth when I was growing up – but rather than the amusements on the front, now I have more fun on the quiet roads nearby.

FROM	Great Yarmouth
DISTANCE	65 miles
ALLOW	1 hr 55 mins

Starting station: Asda, Acle New Road, Great Yarmouth NR30 1SF

MILE	LOCATION	TURN	ON	TO	FOR
0	Great Yarmouth		A149	**Caister**	3
3	Caister bypass		minor	**Hembsy**	16
19	Stalham		A149	**Great Yarmouth**	6
25	Potter Heigham		A1062	**Wroxham**	7.5
32.5	Hoveton		A1151	**Norwich**	1
33.5	Wroxham		B1140	**Acle**	2
35.5	Salhouse		B1140	**Fairhaven**	2.5
38	Panxworth		B1140	**Great Yarmouth**	3
41	B1140		A47	**Great Yarmouth**	1.5
42.5	A47 Acle exit		minor	**Reedham**	0.5
43	Acle		minor	**Reedham**	6
49	Reedham ferry		minor	**Thorpe**	4
53	B1135 junction		B1136	**Great Yarmouth**	2
55	Haddiscoe		A143	**Great Yarmouth**	10
65	Great Yarmouth				

LEEDS

KINGSTON
UPON HULL

48

LIVERPOOL   MANCHESTER

47

SHEFFIELD

50

LINCOLN

STOKE-ON-TRENT

49

46

NOTTINGHAM

SHREWSBURY

42

LEICESTER

45

38

43

44

PETERBOROUGH

BIRMINGHAM

40

41

39

CAMBRIDGE

36   37

35

GLOUCESTER

OXFORD

CARDIFF

BRISTOL

LONDON

England – Midlands

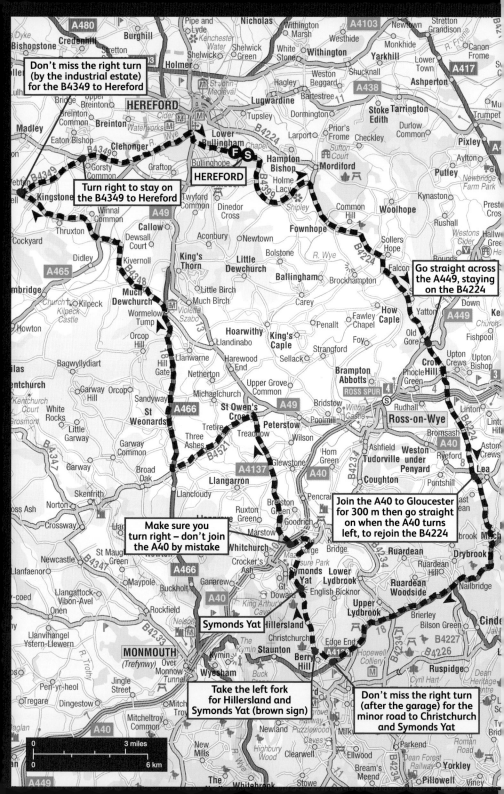

35 Hereford Rideout

The Forest of Dean and the Wye Valley are stunningly unspoilt – though there are roads! This route skirts the edge of the forest, heading over Symonds Yat on its way back to Hereford on some brilliant B-roads.

FROM	Hereford
DISTANCE	58 miles
ALLOW	1 hr 40 mins

Starting station: BP, The Straight Mile, Holme Lacy Road, Hereford HR2 6BQ

MILE	LOCATION	TURN	ON	TO	FOR
0	Hereford	↱ ⟳	B4399	**Holme Lacy**	4
4	B4224 T-junction	↱	B4224	**Ross-on-Wye**	8
12	Upton Bishop	↱	B4224	**Ross**	3
15	A40	↑ ↑	B4224	**Mitcheldean**	2
17	T-junction	↱	B4224	**Mitcheldean**	0.5
17.5	Mitcheldean	⟡→	A4136	**Monmouth**	8
25.5	Berry Hill	↱	minor	**Christchurch**	0.5
26	Berry Hill	↑	minor	**Hillersland**	4
30	B4229 T-junction	↰	B4229	**Hereford (A4137)**	0.5
30.5	A4137 T-junction	↱	A4137	**Hereford**	4.5
35	St Owen's Cross	↰	B4521	**Abergavenny**	3
38	A466 crossroads	+→	A466	**Wormelow**	5.5
43.5	Wormelow	↑	B4348	**Hay-on-Wye**	3.5
47	A465 junction	⊥	B4348	**Peterchurch**	3
50	B4348	↱	B4349	**Hereford**	4.5
54.5	A465	↰	A465	**Hereford**	3.5
58	Hereford				

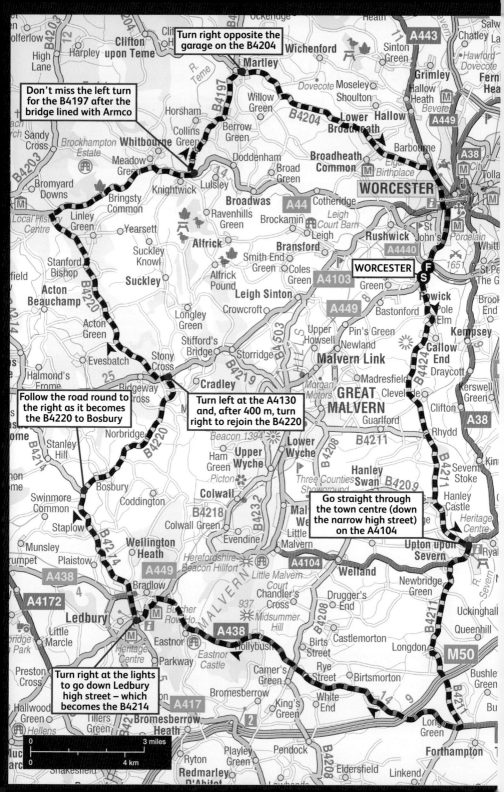

Turn right opposite the garage on the B4204

Don't miss the left turn for the B4197 after the bridge lined with Armco

Follow the road round to the right as it becomes the B4220 to Bosbury

Turn left at the A4130 and, after 400 m, turn right to rejoin the B4220

Go straight through the town centre (down the narrow high street) on the A4104

Turn right at the lights to go down Ledbury high street – which becomes the B4214

36 Worcester Source

If you've ever seen a hillclimb at Shelsley Walsh, you'll know how good the roads in the Malvern Hills can be – and this short rideout from Worcester makes the most of them.

FROM	Worcester
DISTANCE	54.5 miles
ALLOW	1 hr 35 mins

Starting station: Murco, Malvern Road, Powick, Worcester WR2 4QR

MILE	LOCATION	TURN	ON	TO	FOR
0	Worcester	↰ ↱	B4424	**Upton**	7.5
7.5	Upton upon Severn	⭕	A4104	**Little Malvern**	1
8.5	Upton	↰	B4211	**Gloucester**	4.5
13	A438 T-junction	↱	A438	**Ledbury**	5.5
18.5	B2408 junction	↟	A438	**Ledbury**	4.5
23	A449 T-junction	↰	A449	**Ledbury**	1
24	Ledbury	🚦➡	B4214	**Town centre**	8
32	A4130 T-junction	↰ ↱	B4220	**Bromyard**	5.5
37.5	A44 T-junction	↱	A44	**Worcester**	4.5
42	A44	↰	B4197	**Martley**	3.5
45.5	Martley	↱	B4204	**Worcester**	9
54.5	Worcester				

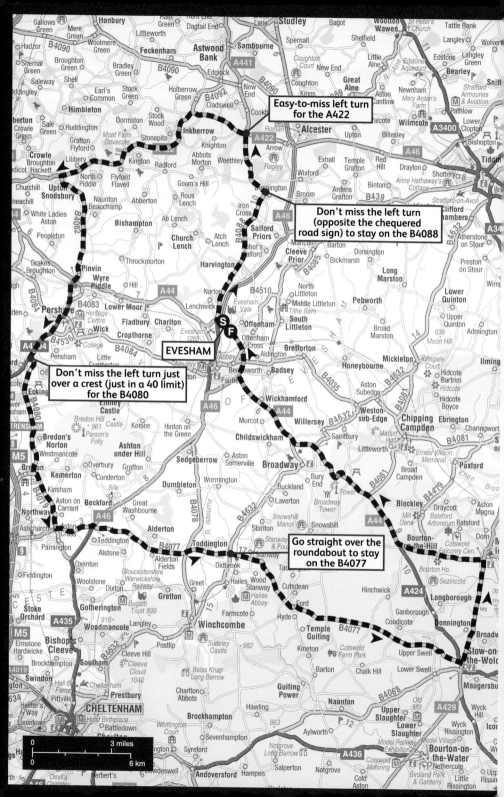

Easy-to-miss left turn
for the A422

Don't miss the left turn
(opposite the chequered
road sign) to stay on the B4088

Don't miss the left turn just
over a crest (just in a 40 limit)
for the B4080

Go straight over the
roundabout to stay
on the B4077

EVESHAM

37 Evesham 69

I think we can all agree that the riding in the Cotswolds is great – with flowing roads through classic English countryside. This relaxed ride breaks out from the Vale of Evesham and is as scenic as it is good to ride.

FROM	Evesham
DISTANCE	69 miles
ALLOW	1 hr 45 mins

Starting station: Texaco Twyford Services, A46, Evesham WR11 4TP

MILE	LOCATION	TURN	ON	TO	FOR
0	Evesham		B4088	**Harvington**	5.5
5.5	B4088		B4088	**Redditch**	2.5
8	B4088/A441		A422	**Worcester**	8.5
16.5	Upton Snodsbury		B4082	**Pershore**	4.5
21	Pinvin		A4104	**Pershore**	1.5
22.5	Pershore		A4104	**Upton**	2
24.5	A4104		B4080	**Tewkesbury**	4.5
29	Bredon		B4079	**Cheltenham**	2.5
31.5	Aston Cross		A46	**Evesham**	1.5
33	Teddington r'bout		B4077	**Stow**	16
49	Stow-on-the-Wold		A429	**Stratford**	4
53	Moreton-in-Marsh		A44	**Evesham**	9
62	Broadway		A44	**Evesham**	7
69	Evesham				

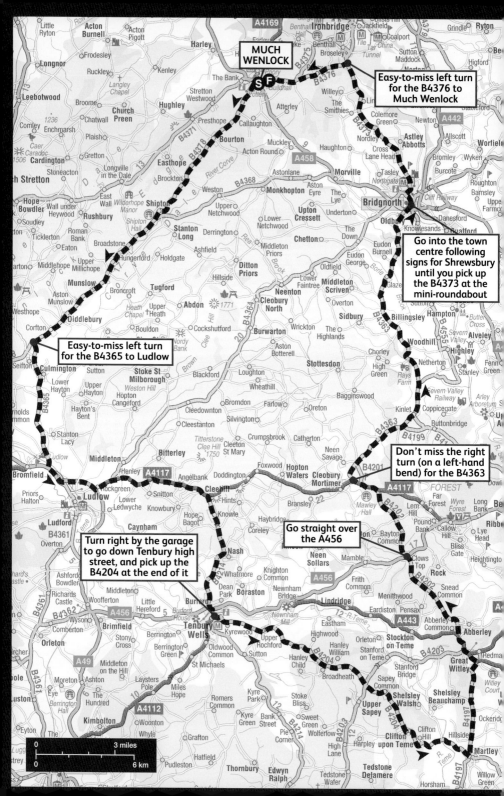

38 Much Ado about Wenlock

There's so much good riding in the Shropshire and Worcestershire hills that even this fairly long rideout can barely scratch the surface.

FROM	Much Wenlock
DISTANCE	78 miles
ALLOW	1 hr 55 mins

Starting station: Shell, Bridgnorth Road, Much Wenlock TF13 6AG

MILE	LOCATION	TURN	ON	TO	FOR
0	Much Wenlock	⌐→ ←⌐	B4378	**Craven Arms**	6.5
6.5	Shipton	⌐→	B4368	**Craven Arms**	6.5
13	B4368	←⌐	B4365	**Ludlow**	5
18	A49 T-junction	←⌐	A49	**Leominster**	2
20	Ludlow bypass	←◯→	A4117	**Kidderminster**	5
25	Cleehill	⌐→	B4214	**Tenbury**	4.5
29.5	Tenbury Wells	←⌐ ⌐→	A456	**Town centre**	0.5
30	Tenbury high st	←⌐	B4204	**Clifton**	12.5
42.5	Martley	←⌐	B4197	**Stourport**	4
46.5	Great Witley	←⌐	A443	**Tenbury**	1
47.5	Abberley	↑	B4202	**Cleobury M'mer**	6.5
54	A4117 T-junction	←⌐	A4117	**Cleobury M'mer**	1
55	A4117	⌐→	B4363	**Bridgnorth**	13
68	Bridgnorth	←⌐ ◯→	B4373	**Broseley**	6
74	B4373	←⌐	B4376	**Much Wenlock**	4
78	Much Wenlock				

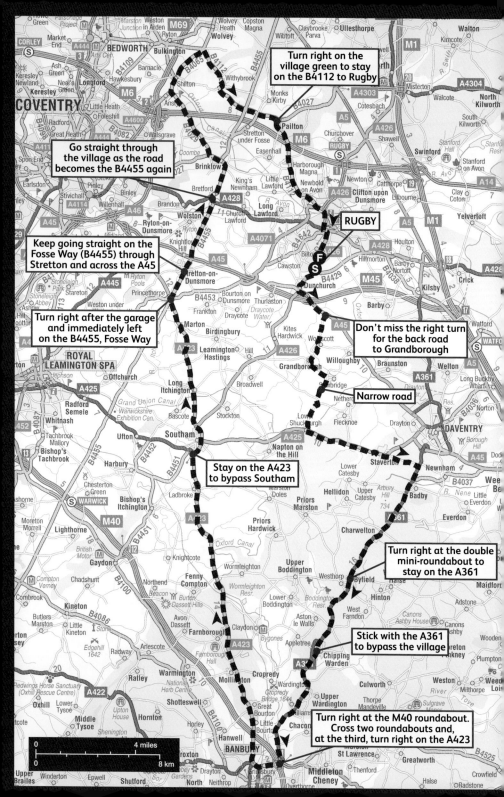

Turn right on the village green to stay on the B4112 to Rugby

Go straight through the village as the road becomes the B4455 again

Keep going straight on the Fosse Way (B4455) through Stretton and across the A45

Turn right after the garage and immediately left on the B4455, Fosse Way

RUGBY

Don't miss the right turn for the back road to Grandborough

Narrow road

Stay on the A423 to bypass Southam

Turn right at the double mini-roundabout to stay on the A361

Stick with the A361 to bypass the village

Turn right at the M40 roundabout. Cross two roundabouts and, at the third, turn right on the A423

0   4 miles
0   8 km

39 Rugby Rideout

I'm indebted to my friend Matthew for showing me some of his favourite back roads, which keep this route around Rugby off some of the major roads. Tackle it yourself

FROM	Rugby
DISTANCE	71 miles
ALLOW	2 hrs 5 mins

Starting station: Sainsbury's, 385 Dunchurch Road, Rugby CV22 6HU

MILE	LOCATION	TURN	ON	TO	FOR
0	Rugby	←◇ ◇→	A426	**Dunchurch**	1
1	Dunchurch	↰	B4229	**Daventry**	0.5
1.5	A45/M45 r'bout	◇	A45	**Daventry**	1
2.5	A45	↱	minor	**Grandborough**	4.5
7	T-junction	↱	minor	**Shuckburgh**	1.5
8.5	A425 T-junction	↰	A425	**Daventry**	3.5
12	roundabout	◇	minor	**Newnham**	1
13	A361 T-junction	↱	A361	**Banbury**	14
27	Banbury	◇→ ◇→	A423	**Southam**	20.5
47.5	Princethorpe	↰ ↰	B4455	**Leicester**	4.5
52	A428	↰	A428	**Coventry**	2
54	Brinklow	↑ ↱	B4029	**Nuneaton**	3
57	T-junction	↱	B4029	**Shilton**	0.5
57.5	Shilton	🚦→	B4065	**Wolvey**	2
59.5	Wolvey	↱	B4112	**Rugby**	11.5
71	Rugby				

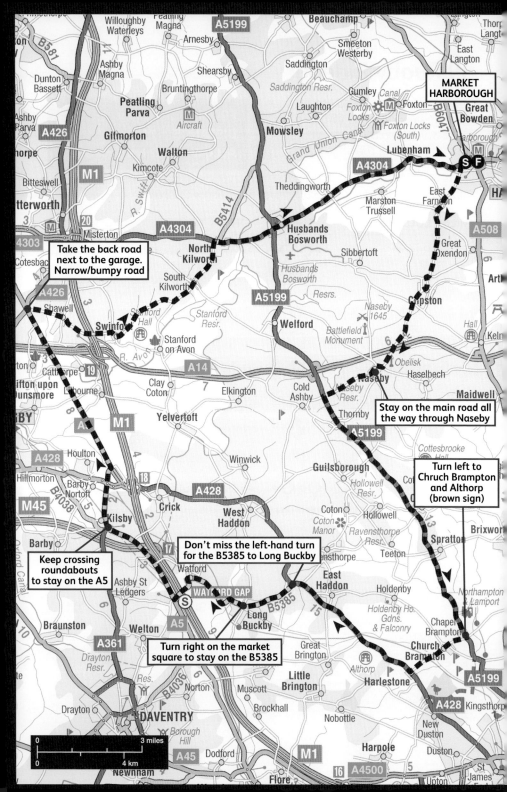

40 Market Harborough Rideout

Like too many other areas, Leicestershire has been blighted by a rash of 50 limits. This route does its best to dodge them, mixing minor roads with one or two large ones to deliver an entertaining ride.

FROM	Market Harborough
DISTANCE	52 miles
ALLOW	1 hr 25 mins

Starting station: Co-op, Coventry Road, Market Harborough LE16 9BZ

MILE	LOCATION	TURN	ON	TO	FOR
0	Market Harborough		minor	**East Farndon**	8.5
8.5	A5199 T-junction		A5199	**Thornby**	8
16.5	Chapel Brampton		minor	**Althorp**	2
18.5	A428 T-junction		A428	**West Haddon**	4
22.5	A428		B5385	**Long Buckby**	2
24.5	Long Buckby		B5385	**Watford**	2.5
27	A5 T-junction		A5	**Nuneaton (M1)**	10
37	Gibbet r'bout		minor	**Shawell**	2.5
39.5	Swinford		minor	**Kilworth**	4.5
44	North Kilworth		A4304	**Mkt Harborough**	8
52	Market Harborough				

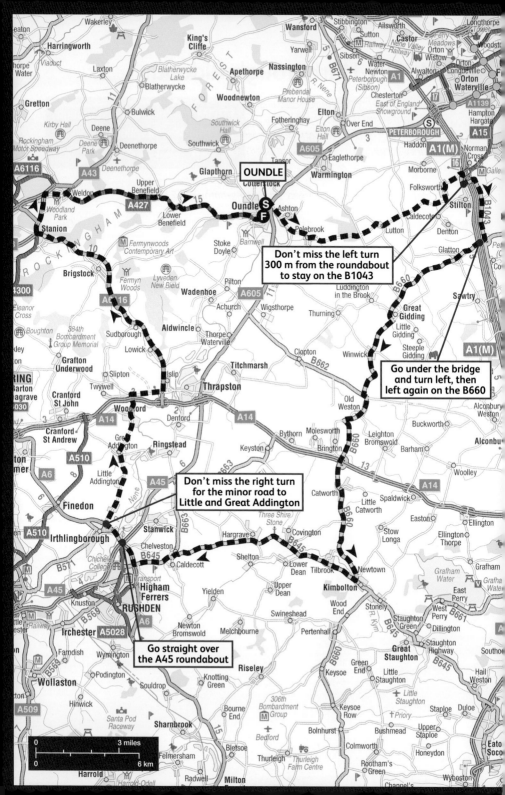

41 Round Oundle

This is another route that uses lots of roads frequently used for photoshoots for Bike, RiDE and MCN – quiet roads with cracking corners. One or two straight roads are used to link them together. It's a cracking ride.

FROM	Oundle
DISTANCE	63 miles
ALLOW	1 hr 45 mins

Starting station: Gulf, New Road, Oundle, Peterborough PE8 4DB

MILE	LOCATION	TURN	ON	TO	FOR
0	Oundle	↱ ⊙	minor	**Ashton**	8
8	T-junction	↰	minor	**Folksworth**	1
9	Norman Cross	⊙ ↰	B1043	**Stilton**	3
12	B1043	↰ ↰	B660	**Glatton**	8
20	T-junction	↰	B660	**Old Weston**	1.5
21.5	B660	↰	B660	**Catworth**	6
27.5	Kimbolton	↱	B645	**Northampton**	9
36.5	A6 roundabout	⊙→ ⊙	A6	**Kettering**	2
38.5	Irthlingborough	↱	minor	**Lt & Gt Addington**	4.5
43	T-junction	↱	minor	**Islip**	1.5
44.5	roundabout	←⊙	A6116	**Corby**	8
52.5	roundabout	⊙→ ⊙	A43	**Corby**	1.5
54	roundabout	⊙→	minor	**Weldon**	0.5
54.5	Weldon	↱	A427	**Oundle**	8.5
63	Oundle				

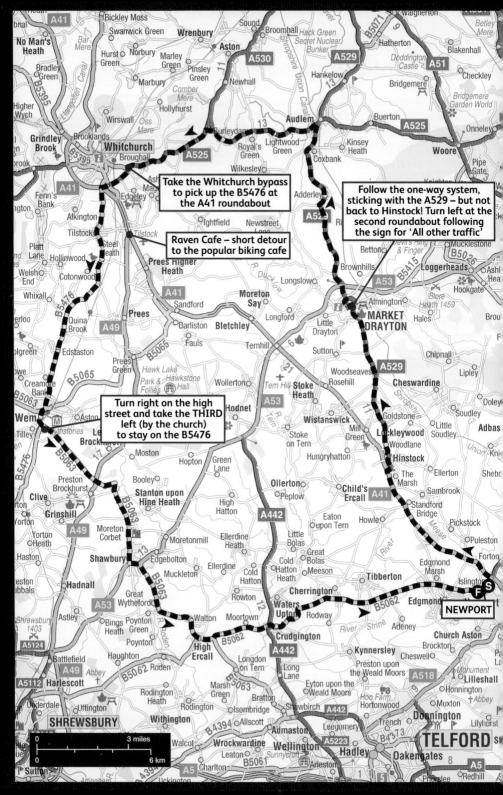

42 'Not <u>That</u> Newport' Rideout

This route does have to pick its way through the towns of Wem and Market Drayton, but it's worth it for the quiet country roads. If you want a drink halfway round, it's a short detour to The Raven at Whitchurch.

FROM	Newport, Shrops
DISTANCE	54.5 miles
ALLOW	1 hr 25 mins

Starting station: Gulf, Forton Road, Newport TF10 7JP

MILE	LOCATION	TURN	ON	TO	FOR
0	Newport		A41	**Whitchurch**	5.5
5.5	A41		A529	**Hinstock**	0.5
6	Hinstock		A529	**Market Drayton**	5
11	Market Drayton		A529	**All other traffic**	1
12	Market Drayton		A529	**Audlem**	6
18	Audlem		A525	**Whitchurch**	4
22	T-junction		A525	**Whitchurch**	4
26	Whitchurch		B5476	**Wem**	8
34	Wem		B5476	**Ellesmere**	0.5
34.5	Wem		B5063	**Shawbury**	2.5
37	A49		B5063	**Shawbury**	3.5
40.5	Shawbury		B5063	**Telford**	4
44.5	roundabout		B5062	**Newport**	2
46.5	A442		B5062	**Newport**	8
54.5	Newport				

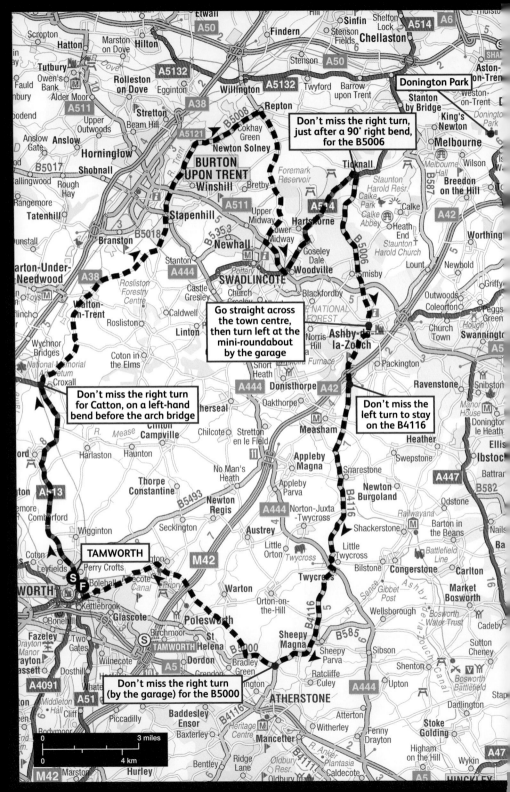

43 Tamworth Rideout

The West Midlands can be busy, but there's still some cracking riding once you get out of the towns – as this laid-back ride from Tamworth demonstrates.

FROM	Tamworth
DISTANCE	53.5 miles
ALLOW	1 hr 45 mins

Starting station: BP, Upper Gungate, Tamworth B79 7NU

MILE	LOCATION	TURN	ON	TO	FOR
0	Tamworth		A513	**Burton**	6.5
6.5	A513		minor	**Catton**	7.5
14	Burton		B5008	**Repton**	4
18	Repton		minor	**Ashby**	5.5
23.5	Midway		A511	**Leicester**	1
24.5	Woodville		A514	**Derby**	4
28.5	Ticknall		B5006	**Ashby**	3.5
32	A511 roundabout		B5006	**Ashby**	1
33	Ashby-d-l-Zouch		B5006	**Town centre**	0.5
33.5	Ashby-d-l-Zouch		B5006	**M42**	1.5
35	A42 junction		B4116	**Measham**	0.5
35.5	B4116		B4116	**Twycross**	5.5
41	Twycross		B4116	**Atherstone**	4
45	B4116		B5000	**Polesworth**	1
46	Grendon		minor	**Warton**	7.5
53.5	Tamworth				

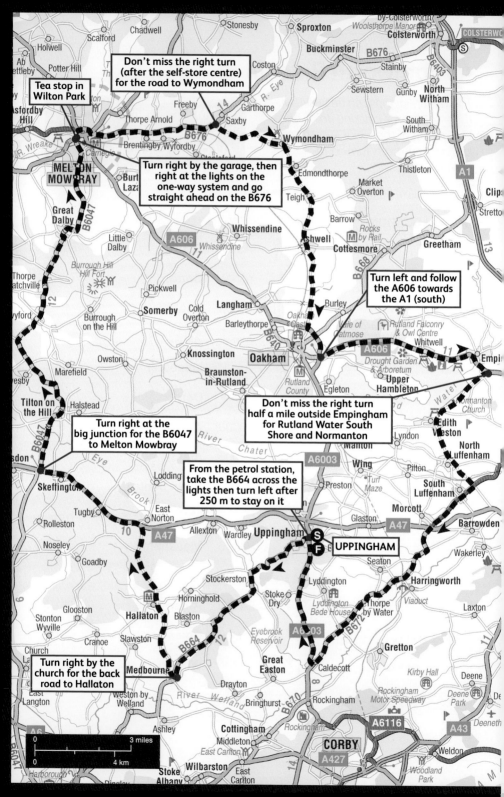

Don't miss the right turn (after the self-store centre) for the road to Wymondham

Tea stop in Wilton Park

Turn right by the garage, then right at the lights on the one-way system and go straight ahead on the B676

Turn left and follow the A606 towards the A1 (south)

Don't miss the right turn half a mile outside Empingham for Rutland Water South Shore and Normanton

Turn right at the big junction for the B6047 to Melton Mowbray

From the petrol station, take the B664 across the lights then turn left after 250 m to stay on it

Turn right by the church for the back road to Hallaton

UPPINGHAM

44 Uppingham Route

When I lived in Lincolnshire and worked in Peterborough, these roads were regularly used for my weekend rideouts... and for more than a few magazine photoshoots. They're simply brilliant: scenic and great to ride.

FROM	Uppingham
DISTANCE	64 miles
ALLOW	1 hr 45 mins

Starting station: BP, 9 North Street East, Uppingham, Oakham LE15 9RN

MILE	LOCATION	TURN	ON	TO	FOR
0	Uppingham		B664	**Mkt Harborough**	7
7	Medbourne		minor	**Hallaton**	2.5
9.5	Hallaton		minor	**East Norton**	2.5
12	A47 T-junction		A47	**Leicester**	3.5
15.5	A47		B6047	**Melton Mowbray**	12
27.5	Melton Mowbray		B676	**Colsterworth**	5
32.5	B676		minor	**Wymondham**	2.5
35	Wymondham		minor	**Edmondthorpe**	6
41	Oakham		A606	**Stamford**	6.5
47.5	A606		minor	**Normanton**	2.5
50	Edith Weston		minor	**Luffenham**	2
52	Wireless Hill		A6121	**Leicester**	2
54	Morcott		B672	**Caldecott**	2
56	T-junction		B672	**Caldecott**	4
60	Caldecott		A6003	**Uppingham**	4
64	Uppingham				

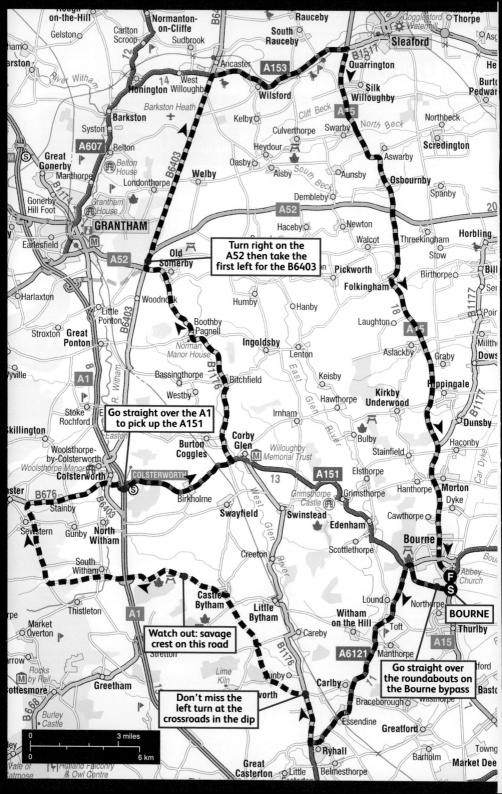

45 Bourne Again

I lived in Bourne for a while and loved riding these roads. This route mixes up challenging minor roads with brilliant A-roads and B-roads for a demanding but rewarding ride. Just keep an eye on the road surfaces on the back roads.

FROM	Bourne
DISTANCE	66 miles
ALLOW	1 hr 40 mins

Starting station: Texaco, Milestone Road, Bourne PE10 0DY

MILE	LOCATION	TURN	ON	TO	FOR
0	Bourne	↑	A151	**Grantham**	2
2	A151	↰	A6121	**Toft**	6.5
8.5	Ryhall	↱	B1176	**Careby**	1.5
10	B1176	↰	minor	**Holywell**	10
20	T-junction	↱	minor	**Sewstern**	2.5
22.5	B676 crossroads	↦	B676	**Colsterworth**	3.5
26	Colsterworth	⊙↦ ⊙↦	A151	**Bourne**	4
30	A151	↰	B1176	**Burton Coggles**	7.5
37.5	A52 roundabout	⊙↦ ↰	B6403	**Ancaster**	6
43.5	Ancaster	🚦↦	A153	**Sleaford**	4.5
48	A15 roundabout	⊙↦	A15	**Peterborough**	6
54	A52 roundabout	↑⊙	A15	**Peterborough**	12
66	Bourne				

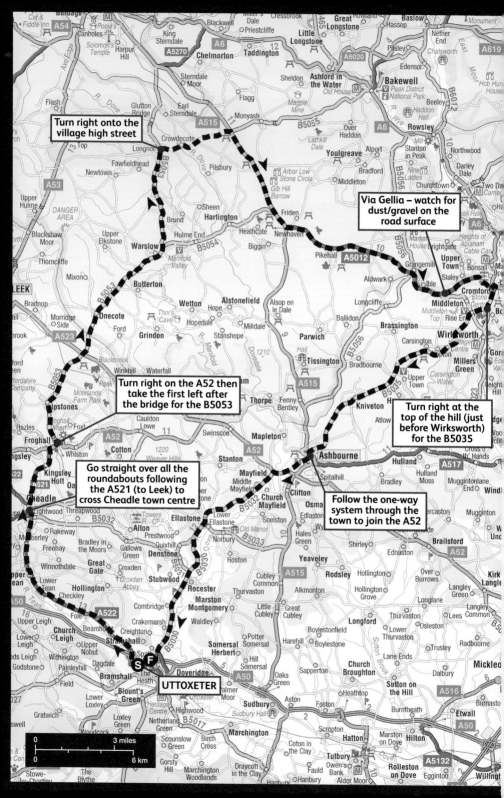

Turn right onto the village high street

Via Gellia – watch for dust/gravel on the road surface

Turn right on the A52 then take the first left after the bridge for the B5053

Turn right at the top of the hill (just before Wirksworth) for the B5035

Go straight over all the roundabouts following the A521 (to Leek) to cross Cheadle town centre

Follow the one-way system through the town to join the A52

UTTOXETER

0 3 miles

0 6 km

46 Ultimate Uttoxeter

This route could easily have run from biker hotspot Matlock Bath – and it's an easy detour from Cromford – but I prefer to keep to the quieter roads when I can. Just take care on the Via Gellia, the A5012.

FROM	Uttoxeter
DISTANCE	64 miles
ALLOW	1 hr 50 mins

Starting station: Shell, New Road, Uttoxeter ST14 7DB

MILE	LOCATION	TURN	ON	TO	FOR
0	Uttoxeter	↱ ⟳→	A522	**Cheadle**	5.5
5.5	Upper Tean	↱	A522	**Cheadle**	3
8.5	Cheadle	↱	A521	**Ashbourne**	3
11.5	Froghall	↱ ↰	B5053	**Ipstones**	4
15.5	A523 crossroads	✛	B5053	**Onecote**	9
24.5	Longnor	↱	minor	**Crowdecote**	3.5
28	A515 T-junction	↱	A515	**Ashbourne**	4
32	Newhaven	↰	A5012	**Cromford**	9.5
41.5	Cromford	↱	B5036	**Middleton**	1
42.5	Wirksworth	↱	B5035	**Ashbourne**	9.5
52	Ashbourne	↰	A515	**Town centre**	1
53	Ashbourne	⟳→	A52	**Leek**	1
54	Mayfield	↰	B5032	**Uttoxeter**	6
60	Rocester	⟳↑	B5030	**Uttoxeter**	4
64	Uttoxeter				

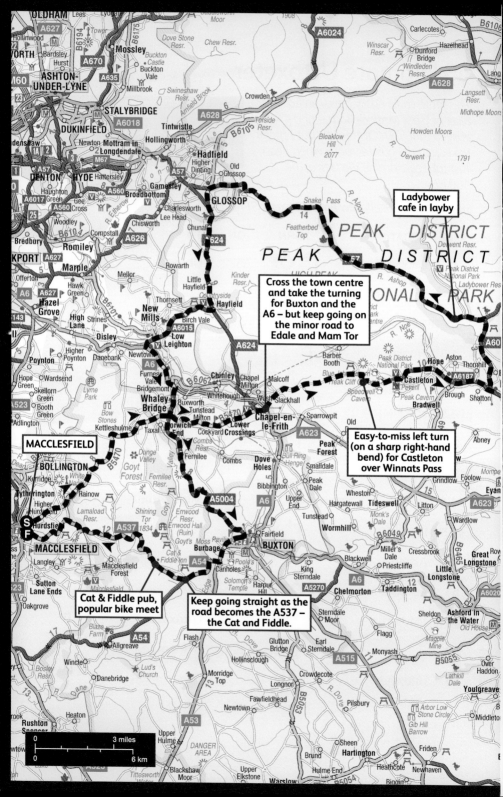

Ladybower cafe in layby

Cross the town centre and take the turning for Buxton and the A6 – but keep going on the minor road to Edale and Mam Tor

Easy-to-miss left turn (on a sharp right-hand bend) for Castleton over Winnats Pass

MACCLESFIELD

Cat & Fiddle pub, popular bike meet

Keep going straight as the road becomes the A537 – the Cat and Fiddle.

0   3 miles
0   6 km

47 Cat n Fiddle Figure-of-Eight

This route shows both the best and worst aspects of the Peak District. The best bits are the scenery and flowing roads; the worst are the lowered limits and occasional bursts of traffic. It's still a stunning ride though.

FROM	Macclesfield
DISTANCE	68.5 miles
ALLOW	2 hrs

Starting station: Tesco, Hibel Road, Macclesfield SK10 2AB

MILE	LOCATION	TURN	ON	TO	FOR
0	Macclesfield	↱ ←	B5470	**Chapel-en-le-Frith**	12
12	Chapel-en-le-Frith	↰	minor	**Edale**	4.5
16.5	minor road	↰	minor	**Castleton**	1
17.5	T-junction	↱	minor	**Castleton**	4.5
22	Hope Valley	←	A6013	**Bamford**	3
25	Ladybower Reservoir	←	A57	**Manchester**	13.5
38.5	Glossop	←	A624	**Chapel-en-le-Frith**	5
43.5	Hayfield	↱	A6015	**New Mills**	3
46.5	A6 T-junction	←	A6	**Buxton**	2
48.5	A6 roundabout	⟳→	B5470	**Macclesfield**	1
49.5	Whaley Bridge	↑	A5004	**Buxton**	7
56.5	Buxton	↱	A53	**Leek**	1.5
58	Buxton	↱	A54	**Congleton**	2
60	A54	↱	A537	**Macclesfield**	8.5
68.5	Macclesfield				

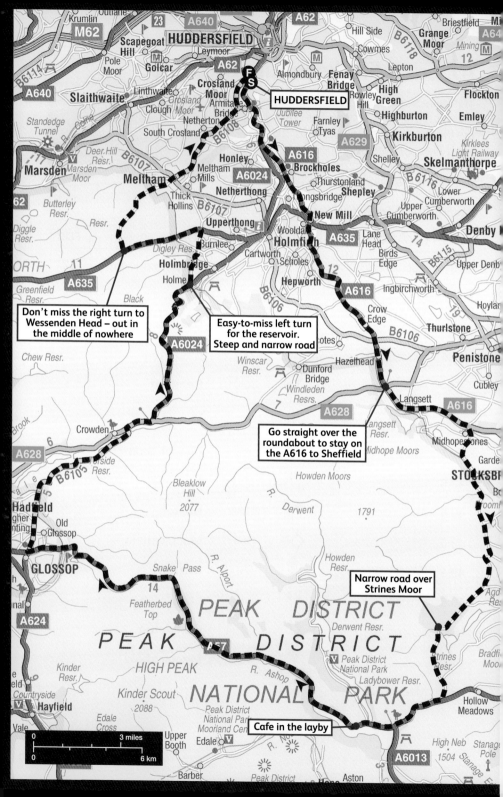

48 Snake Pass and Holm Moss

Three of my favourite roads in the Peak District are on this relaxed rideout: the broad and epic Snake Pass; majestic Holm Moss; and the narrow, challenging Strines Moor Road.

FROM	Huddersfield
DISTANCE	60.5 miles
ALLOW	1 hr 40 mins

Starting station: Shell, Woodhead Road, Lockwood, Huddersfield HD4 6EP

MILE	LOCATION	TURN	ON	TO	FOR
0	Huddersfield	↱	A616	**Holmfirth**	5
5	New Mill crossroads	✛	A616	**Sheffield**	8.5
13.5	Midhopestones	↱	minor	**Bradfield**	9.5
23	A57 T-junction	↱	A57	**Bamford**	15.5
38.5	Glossop	🚦↱	B1605	**Barnsley**	5.5
44	A628 T-junction	↱	A628	**Barnsley**	0.5
44.5	Woodhead Reservoir	↰	A6204	**Holmfirth**	5
49.5	Holme	⋎	minor	**Digley Reservoir**	1.5
51	The Ford Inn	↰	A635	**Greenfield**	2.5
53.5	A653	↱	minor	**Wessenden Head**	3
56.5	Meltham	✛	B6108	**Huddersfield**	4
60.5	Huddersfield				

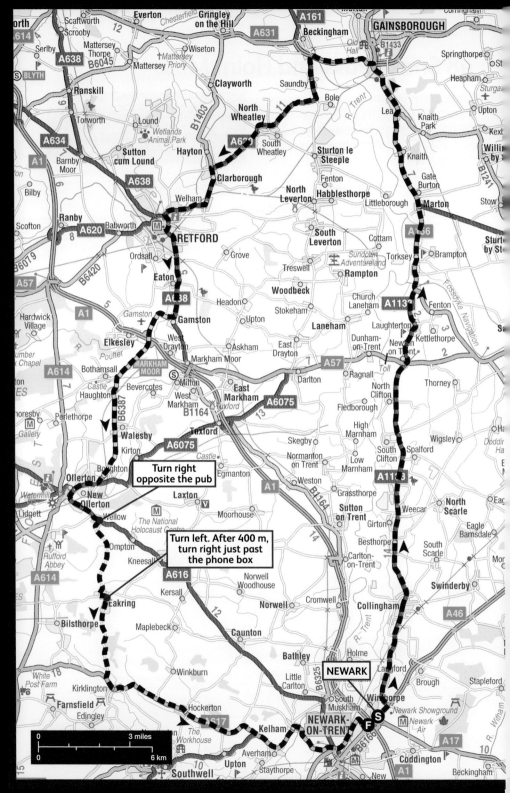

Turn right opposite the pub

Turn left. After 400 m, turn right just past the phone box

49 Trent Country Loop

From Newark to Gainsborough, this route roughly follows the course of the River Trent, then loops off on some high-quality minor roads for a great afternoon's ride.

FROM	Newark
DISTANCE	60.5 miles
ALLOW	1 hr 40 mins

Starting station: Esso, A46 Lincoln Road, Winthorpe, Newark NG24 2DF

MILE	LOCATION	TURN	ON	TO	FOR
0	Newark		A1133	**Gainsborough**	12
12	A57		A1133	**Gainsborough**	2.5
14.5	Torksey Lock		A156	**Gainsborough**	7
21.5	Gainsborough		A631	**Rotherham**	2.5
24	roundabout		A620	**Retford**	1.5
25.5	roundabout		A620	**Retford**	7
32.5	Retford		A638	**Lincoln**	3.5
36	Gamston		B6387	**Ollerton**	6.5
42.5	Boughton		A6057	**Ollerton**	1
43.5	Ollerton		A616	**Newark**	1.5
45	Wellow		minor	**Eakring**	2.5
47.5	Eakring		minor	**National Grid**	3
50.5	A617 T-junction		A617	**Newark**	10
60.5	Newark				

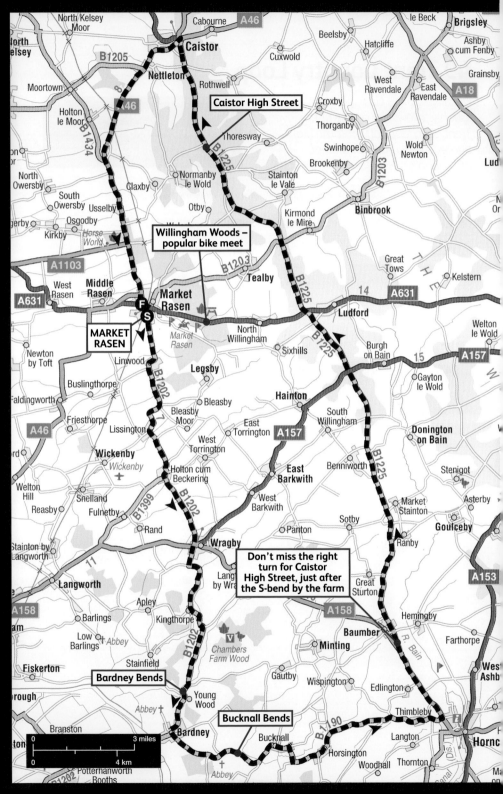

50 Rasen Shine

North Lincolnshire has some of England's finest roads – mostly packed into this route. Bardney Bends, Bucknall Bends or Caistor High Street would make any rideout great... all three are on this awesome route.

FROM	Market Rasen
DISTANCE	55.5 miles
ALLOW	1 hr 15 mins

Starting station: Tesco, Linwood Road, Market Rasen LN8 3AW

MILE	LOCATION	TURN	ON	TO	FOR
0	Market Rasen	↱	B1202	**Wragby**	8
8	Wragby	🚦	B1202	**Bardney**	6
14	Bardney	↑	B1190	**Horncastle**	10
24	Horncastle	↰	A158	**Baumber**	2.5
26.5	A158	↱	B1225	**Caistor**	8.5
35	A157	✛	B1225	**Caistor**	2
37	A631	✛	B1225	**Caistor**	2
39	B1203	✛	B1225	**Caistor**	7.5
46.5	Caistor	↰	A46	**Lincoln**	9
55.5	Market Rasen				

England – North

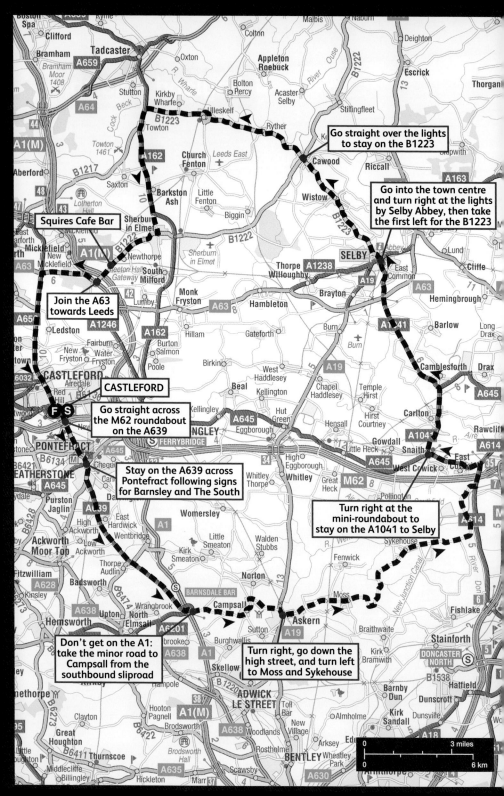

51 Castleford Rideout

This route is built around visiting the famous Squires Cafe, but there's no need to take the direct route. There's awesome riding, though the towns of Pontefract and Selby also need to be crossed.

FROM	Castleford
DISTANCE	57.5 miles
ALLOW	1 hr 45 mins

Starting station: BP, Park Road, Castleford WF10 4RJ

MILE	LOCATION	TURN	ON	TO	FOR
0	Castleford	↱	A639	**Pontefract**	8
8	Barnsdale Bar	↰	A1 S	**A1 (South)**	200 m
8	sliproad	↰	minor	**Campsall**	2.5
10.5	Campsall	↰	minor	**Askern**	1.5
12	Askern	↱ ↰	minor	**Moss**	11
23	A614 T-junction	↰	A614	**Goole**	0.5
23.5	roundabout	↜○	A1041	**Selby**	8
31.5	A63 roundabout	○	A1041	**Town centre**	1
32.5	Selby	⯈ ⯇	B1223	**Cawood**	9
41.5	Ulleskelf	↱	B1223	**Tadcaster**	2.5
44	A162 T-junction	↰	A162	**Towton**	3.5
47.5	roundabout	○	minor	**Sherburn in Elmet**	0.5
48	Sherburn	⯈	B1222	**Leeds**	3
51	A63 roundabout	○	A63	**Leeds**	2
53	roundabout	↜○	A656	**Castleford**	4.5
57.5	Castleford				

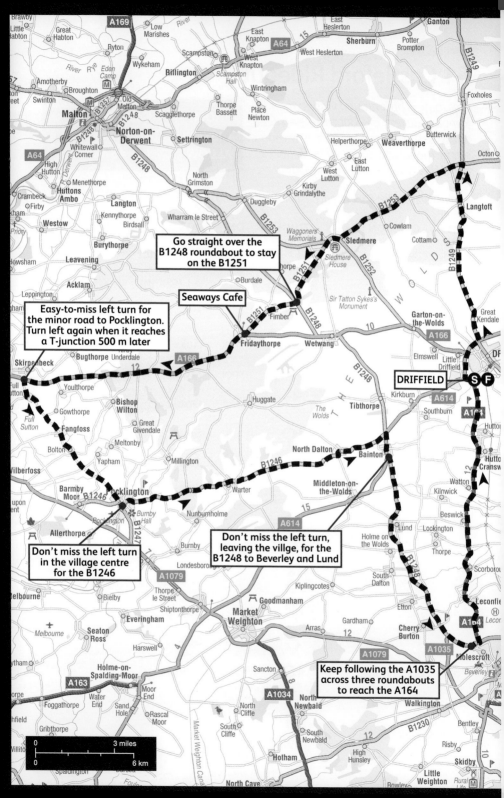

Go straight over the B1248 roundabout to stay on the B1251

Seaways Cafe

Easy-to-miss left turn for the minor road to Pocklington. Turn left again when it reaches a T-junction 500 m later

DRIFFIELD

Don't miss the left turn, leaving the villge, for the B1248 to Beverley and Lund

Don't miss the left turn in the village centre for the B1246

Keep following the A1035 across three roundabouts to reach the A164

52 High Wolds, Driffield

There's some fantastic riding in the Wolds of Humberside. This route uses many roads shown to me by my good friend Hoody and includes a stop at his favourite cafe, Seaways in Fridaythorpe. It's great.

FROM	Driffield
DISTANCE	66 miles
ALLOW	1 hr 35 mins

Starting station: JET, Beverley Road, Driffield YO25 6RX

MILE	LOCATION	TURN	ON	TO	FOR
0	Driffield		A164	**Bridlington (A614)**	0.5
0.5	Driffield bypass		A614	**Bridlington**	1.5
2	Driffield bypass		B1249	**Scarborough**	7
9	roundabout		B1253	**Sledmere**	5.5
14.5	Sledmere		B1251	**Fridaythorpe**	5.5
20	Fridaythorpe		A166	**York**	9
29	A166		minor	**Pocklington**	6
35	Pocklington		B1246	**Driffield**	11
46	roundabout		A614	**Goole (M62)**	1
47	Bainton		B1248	**Beverley**	7.5
54.5	Cherry Burton		A1035	**Bridlington**	1.5
56	Beverley		A164	**Driffield**	10
66	Driffield				

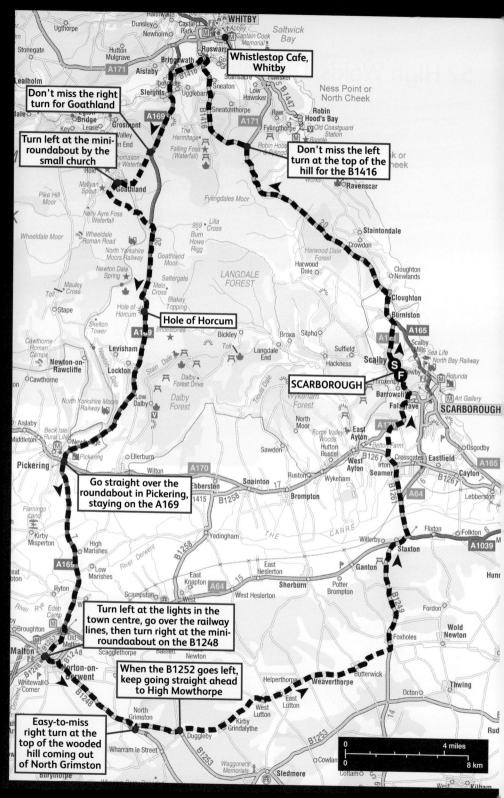

Whistlestop Cafe, Whitby

Don't miss the right turn for Goathland

Turn left at the mini-roundabout by the small church

Don't miss the left turn at the top of the hill for the B1416

Hole of Horcum

SCARBOROUGH

Go straight over the roundabout in Pickering, staying on the A169

Turn left at the lights in the town centre, go over the railway lines, then turn right at the mini-roundabout on the B1248

When the B1252 goes left, keep going straight ahead to High Mowthorpe

Easy-to-miss right turn at the top of the wooded hill coming out of North Grimston

53 Scarborough and Moors

From Scarborough, this route heads out to Whitby (short detour to the excellent Whistlestop Cafe) then out to Goathland. After the wild, open moors, it heads into wolds to avoid sitting on the dull A64.

FROM	Scarborough
DISTANCE	76.5 miles
ALLOW	2 hrs

Starting station: JET, Scalby Road, Scarborough YO12 6UA

MILE	LOCATION	TURN	ON	TO	FOR
0	Scarborough	↱	A171	**Whitby**	12
12	A171	↰	B1416	**Ruswarp**	4.5
16.5	Ruswarp	↰	B1410	**Sleights**	1.5
18	Sleights	↰	A169	**Pickering**	3.5
21.5	A171	↱	minor	**Goathland**	3
24.5	Goathland	⟳	minor	**Pickering**	2
26.5	A169	↱	A169	**Pickering**	18
44.5	A64 roundabout	⟳	B1257	**Malton**	1.5
46	Malton	🚦←	B1248	**Beverley**	0.5
46.5	Malton	⟳→ ⟳	B1248	**Beverley**	4.5
51	B1248	⋎	B1253	**Driffield**	2
53	Duggleby	⋏	minor	**High Mowthorpe**	9.5
62.5	B1249 junction	↰	B1249	**Foxholes**	4.5
67	Staxton Hill	🚦→ ⟳	A64	**Scarborough**	2
69	roundabout	⟳	B1261	**Seamer**	3
72	East Ayton	⟳→	A170	**Scarborough**	4.5
76.5	Scarborough				

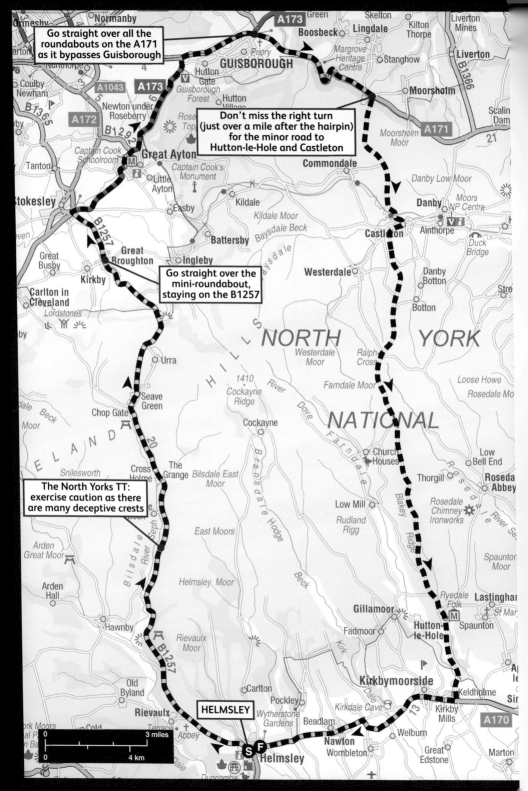

Go straight over all the roundabouts on the A171 as it bypasses Guisborough

Don't miss the right turn (just over a mile after the hairpin) for the minor road to Hutton-le-Hole and Castleton

Go straight over the mini-roundabout, staying on the B1257

The North Yorks TT: exercise caution as there are many deceptive crests

54 North Yorkshire Moors

You can't go wrong with this simplest of runs over the North York Moors. From Helmsley, take the North Yorks TT to Stokesley, then return across the moor top from Castleton to Kirkbymoorside. Simply stunning.

FROM	Helmsley
DISTANCE	58 miles
ALLOW	1 hr 20 mins

Starting station: BATA, Bondgate Garage, Helmsley, York YO62 5EZ

MILE	LOCATION	TURN	ON	TO	FOR
0	Helmsley	↰ ↑	B1257	**Stokesley**	19.5
19.5	Stokesley	⟳→	A173	**Great Ayton**	6
25.5	A171 roundabout	⟳→	A171	**Whitby**	7
32.5	A171	↱	minor	**Hutton-le-Hole**	4
36.5	Castleton	↱	minor	**Westerdale** ⇄	15
51.5	Kirkbymoorside	↱	A170	**Thirsk**	6.5
58	Helmsley				

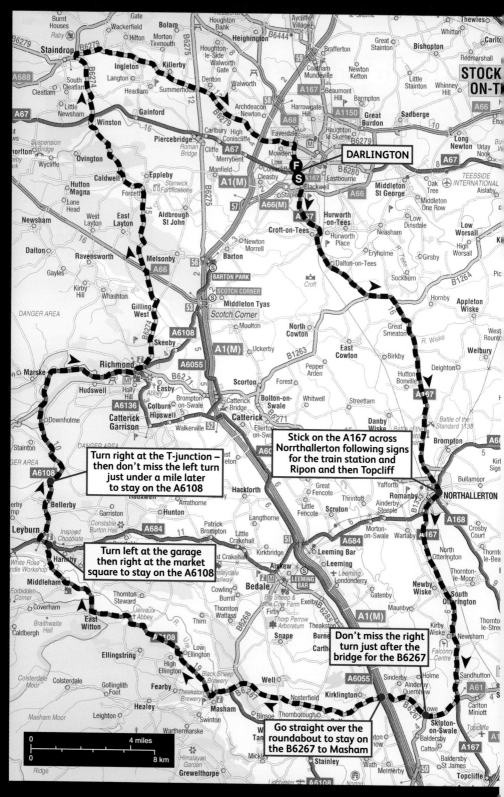

DARLINGTON

Turn right at the T-junction – then don't miss the left turn just under a mile later to stay on the A6108

Stick on the A167 across Norrthallerton following signs for the train station and Ripon and then Topcliff

Turn left at the garage then right at the market square to stay on the A6108

Don't miss the right turn just after the bridge for the B6267

Go straight over the roundabout to stay on the B6267 to Masham

0   4 miles
0   8 km

55 Darlington Rideout

This route around Darlington hops across the great north road – the A1(M) – in search of the great riding that motorway can't deliver. And there's plenty of great riding on these quieter roads heading out to the Dales.

FROM	Darlington
DISTANCE	84 miles
ALLOW	2 hrs 10 mins

Starting station: JET, 1–3 Carmel Road South, Darlington DL3 8DQ

MILE	LOCATION	TURN	ON	TO	FOR
0	Darlington	↰	A67	**Yarm**	0.5
0.5	Darlington	⟳	A167	**Northallerton**	23.5
24	Busby Stoop	⟳	A61	**Ripon**	2
26	Skipton-on-Swale	↱	B6267	**Masham**	9
35	A6108 junction	↑	A6108	**Masham**	9
46	Leyburn	↰ ↱	A6108	**Richmond**	3
49	A6108	↱ ↰	A6108	**Richmond**	8.5
57.5	Richmond	⟲ ⟳	A6108	**Town centre**	0.5
58	Richmond	⟲	B6274	**Gilling West**	4
62	A66	↰	B6274	**East Layton**	7.5
69.5	Winston	↱ ↑	B6274	**Staindrop**	3
72.5	Staindrop	↱ ↱	B6279	**Darlington**	11.5
84	Darlington				

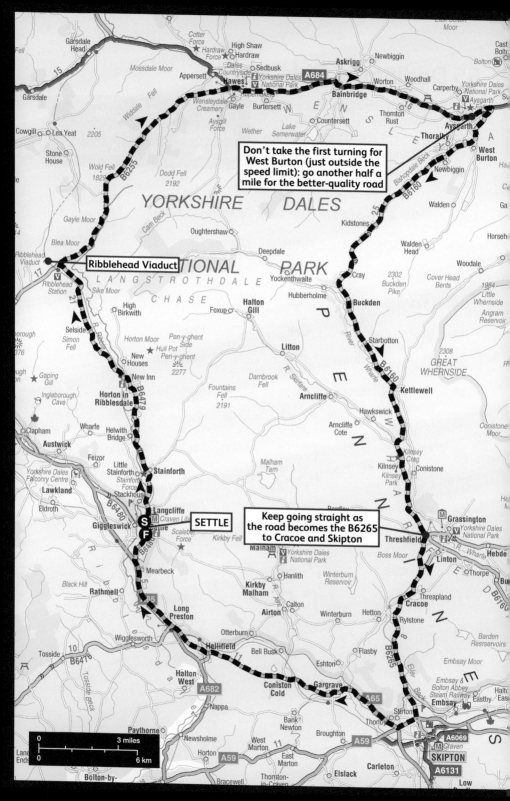

Ribblehead Viaduct

Don't take the first turning for West Burton (just outside the speed limit): go another half a mile for the better-quality road

SETTLE

Keep going straight as the road becomes the B6265 to Cracoe and Skipton

56 Dales Classic

When I was on Bike in the early 2000s, we had a 440-mile test route... largely built as an excuse to come from Peterborough to ride the B6255 through the Dales. This route's a more manageable way to do it.

FROM	Settle
DISTANCE	75 miles
ALLOW	1 hr 35 mins

Starting station: Co-op, 9 Church Street, Settle BD24 9JD

MILE	LOCATION	TURN	ON	TO	FOR
0	Settle	↰ ↱	B6479	**Horton in Ribblesdale**	11.5
11.5	Ribblehead	↱	B6255	**Hawes**	10
21.5	Hawes	↱	A684	**Aysgarth**	4
25.5	Bainbridge	↱	A684	**Aysgarth**	7
32.5	Aysgarth	↱	B6160	**West Burton**	27
59.5	Skipton	⟲→	A65	**Kendal**	1
60.5	Skipton	⟲↗	A65	**The Lakes**	13
73.5	A65 roundabout	⟲→	B6480	**Settle**	1.5
75	Settle				

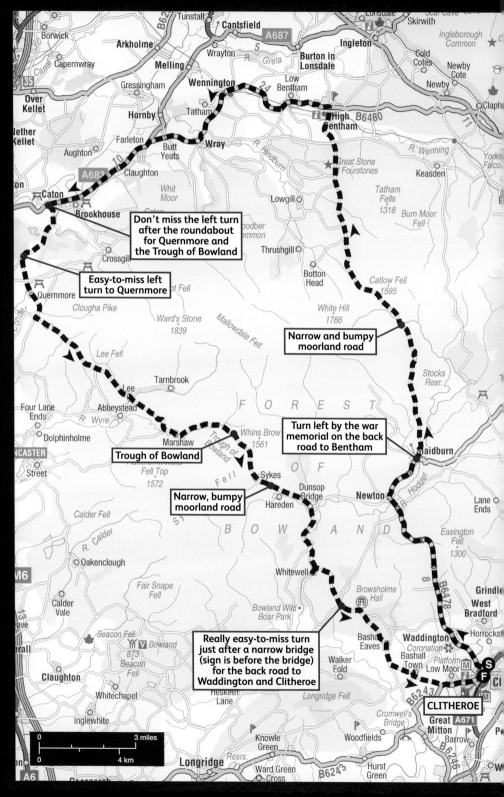

Don't miss the left turn after the roundabout for Quernmore and the Trough of Bowland

Easy-to-miss left turn to Quernmore

Narrow and bumpy moorland road

Turn left by the war memorial on the back road to Bentham

Trough of Bowland

Narrow, bumpy moorland road

Really easy-to-miss turn just after a narrow bridge (sign is before the bridge) for the back road to Waddington and Clitheroe

CLITHEROE

57 Bowland Rideout

If you want a wild, untamed landscape and empty roads, head to the Forest of Bowland. There are some narrow and bumpy roads on this route – it's how you experience the isolation... but take it steady with a pillion.

FROM	Clitheroe
DISTANCE	58.5 miles
ALLOW	1 hr 40 mins

Starting station: BP, Chatburn Road, Clitheroe BB7 2AP

MILE	LOCATION	TURN	ON	TO	FOR
0	Clitheroe	⊙→	B6478	**Waddington**	7
7	Newton-in-Bowland	↱	B6478	**Slaidburn**	1.5
8.5	Slaidburn	↰	minor	**Bentham**	12
20.5	Bentham	↰	B6480	**Lancaster**	7
27.5	A683 T-junction	↰	A683	**Lancaster**	3.5
31	Caton	⊙ ↰	minor	**Quernmore**	2.5
33.5	minor road	⦚	minor	**Quernmore**	2
35.5	Quernmore village crossroads	↰	minor	**Trough of Bowland**	11.5
47	Dunsop Bridge	↱	minor	**Whitewell**	4
51	minor road	↰	minor	**Waddington**	6
57	B6243 T-junction	↰	B6243	**Clitheroe**	1.5
58.5	Clitheroe				

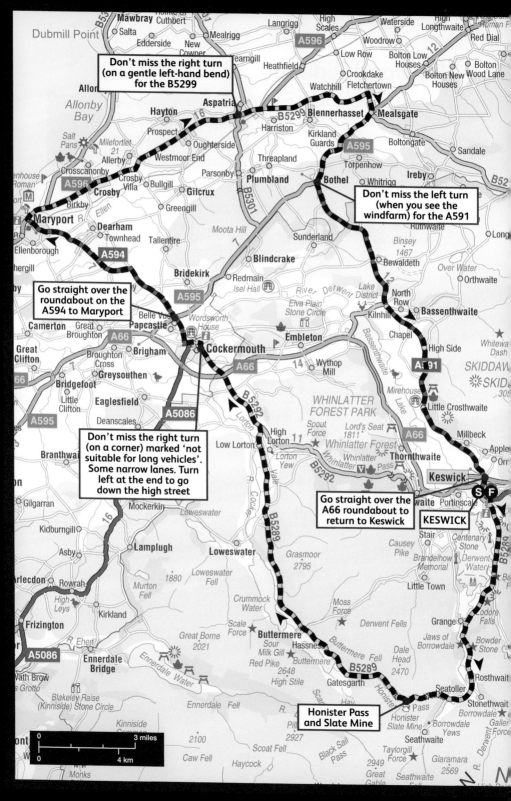

58 Honister Loop

The Lake District is undoubtedly one of the most beautiful corners of the country – but it can get busy. While this route does use the popular Honister Pass, it aims to stay off the beaten track for the rest of it.

FROM	Keswick
DISTANCE	58.5 miles
ALLOW	1 hr 30 mins

Starting station: Shell, Penrith Road, Keswick CA12 4JP

MILE	LOCATION	TURN	ON	TO	FOR
0	Keswick	↰	A5271	**Town centre**	1
1	Keswick	↤⊙	B5289	**Borrowdale**	19
20	T-junction	↱	B5289	**Cockermouth**	3
23	Cockermouth	↱ ↰	minor	**High Street**	0.5
23.5	Cockermouth	⊙ ⊙↦	A594	**Maryport**	7
30.5	Maryport	🚦↦	A596	**Carlisle**	8
38.5	Aspatria	↑	B5299	**Mealsgate**	4.5
43	Mealsgate	↱	A595	**Cockermouth**	3
46	A595	↰	A591	**Keswick**	12.5
58.5	Keswick				

59 Ambleside Rideout

This route does use some popular Lakeland roads – including Kirkstone Pass – with some of the best views in England. It also uses the Windermere ferry, so allow an extra 20 mins for that. It's a lovely, scenic, relaxed ride.

FROM	Ambleside
DISTANCE	58.5 miles
ALLOW	1 hr 30 mins

Starting station: BP, Lake Road, Ambleside LA22 0DF

MILE	LOCATION	TURN	ON	TO	FOR
0	Ambleside	↑ ↱	A591	**Keswick**	11.5
11.5	A591	↟	B5322	**Threlkeld**	4.5
16	A66 T-junction	↱	A66	**Penrith (M6)**	4.5
20.5	A66	↱	A5091	**Troutbeck**	5
25.5	A592 T-junction	↱	A592	**Glenridding**	14.5
40	Windermere	⟳	A592	**Bowness Bay**	2.5
42.5	Windermere ferry	↱🛥	B5285	**Hawkshead**	0.5
43	Sawrey	↑	B5285	**Hawkshead**	4
47	Hawkshead	↱	B5285	**Hawkshead village**	0.5
47.5	Hawkshead	↰	B5285	**Hawkshead Hill**	3.5
51	Coniston	↱	A593	**Ambleside**	7.5
58.5	Ambleside				

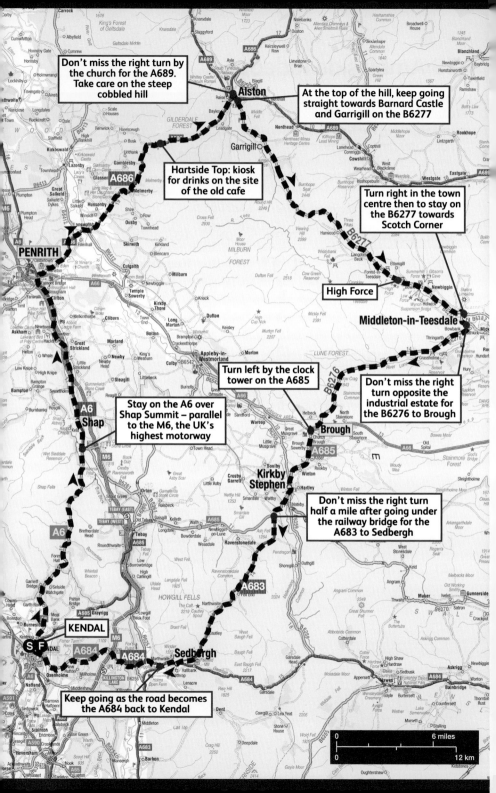

Don't miss the right turn by the church for the A689. Take care on the steep cobbled hill

At the top of the hill, keep going straight towards Barnard Castle and Garrigill on the B6277

Hartside Top: kiosk for drinks on the site of the old cafe

Turn right in the town centre then to stay on the B6277 towards Scotch Corner

High Force

Don't miss the right turn opposite the industrial estate for the B6276 to Brough

Turn left by the clock tower on the A685

Stay on the A6 over Shap Summit – parallel to the M6, the UK's highest motorway

Don't miss the right turn half a mile after going under the railway bridge for the A683 to Sedbergh

Keep going as the road becomes the A684 back to Kendal

0   6 miles

0   12 km

60 Kendal. Mint

This is one of the longer rides in this book, but it's also one of the best. Shap Summit, Hartside Pass, the B6277 and B6276... every road is stunning.

FROM	Kendal
DISTANCE	110 miles
ALLOW	2 hrs 20 mins

Starting station: Sainsbury's, Mint Bridge, Shap Road, Kendal LA9 6DL

MILE	LOCATION	TURN	ON	TO	FOR
0	Kendal	◀🚦	A6	**Shap**	24.5
24.5	Kemplay Bank	⟳	A686	**Alston**	19.5
44	Alston	↱	A689	**Town centre**	0.5
44.5	Alston	⬆	B6277	**Garrigill**	21.5
66	Middleton-in-Teesdale	↱	B6277	**Scotch Corner**	0.5
66.5	B6277	⬆	B6276	**Brough**	13
79.5	T-junction	↱	B6276	**Brough**	0.5
80	Brough	↰	A685	**Kirkby Stephen**	6
86	A685	↰	A683	**Sedbergh**	12
98	Sedbergh	⬆	A684	**Kendal**	12
110	Kendal				

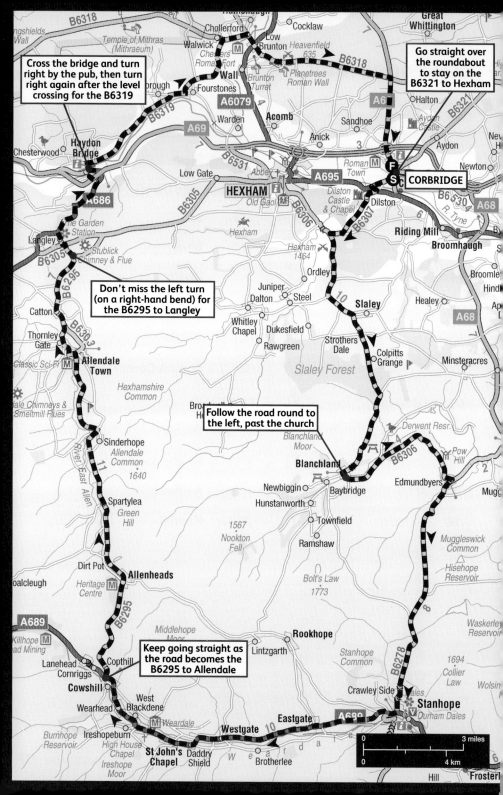

61 Pennine Perfection

There's no such thing as a perfect route, but this ride through the majestic Pennines comes pretty close. On a sunny day, it's hard to imagine a better place to be riding. Just watch out for sheep on the moors.

FROM	Corbridge
DISTANCE	66 miles
ALLOW	1 hr 40 mins

Starting station: Shell, Main Street, Corbridge NE45 5LB

MILE	LOCATION	TURN	ON	TO	FOR
0	Corbridge		B6321	**Hexham**	1
1	B6321		A695	**Prudhoe**	200 m
1	A695		B6307	**Blanchland**	2
3	B6306 T-junction		B6306	**Blanchland**	12.5
15.5	Edmundbyers		B6278	**Stanhope**	7.5
23	Stanhope		A689	**Alston**	24
47	After Allendale		B6295	**Langley**	0.5
47.5	B6305 junction		B6295	**Langley**	0.5
48	A686 T-junction		A686	**Haydon Bridge**	2.5
50.5	A69		A686	**Haydon Bridge**	0.5
51	Haydon Bridge		B6319	**Chollerford**	4
55	Fourstones		B6319	**Chollerford**	2.5
57.5	B6319 T-junction		B6319	**Newcastle**	0.5
58	Chollerford		B6318	**Newcastle**	4.5
62.5	A68 roundabout		A68	**Newcastle**	3.5
66	Corbridge				

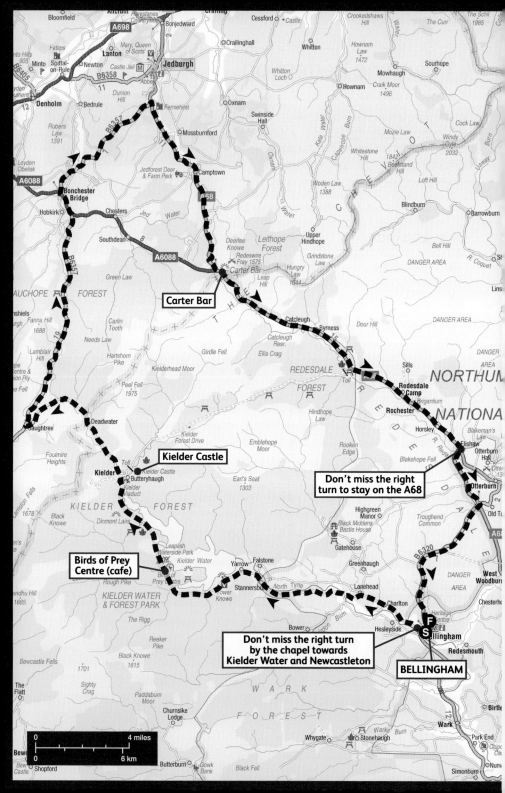

Carter Bar

Kielder Castle

Birds of Prey
Centre (cafe)

Don't miss the right
turn to stay on the A68

Don't miss the right turn
by the chapel towards
Kielder Water and Newcastleton

BELLINGHAM

62 Kielder Instinct

This route heads through Kielder Forest into Scotland, looping back through Carter Bar (obligatory photo) and back to Bellingham on some of the finest riding in England.

FROM	Bellingham
DISTANCE	72.5 miles
ALLOW	1 hr 25 mins

Starting station: Bellingham Garage, Station Road, Bellingham NE48 2BS

MILE	LOCATION	TURN	ON	TO	FOR
0	Bellingham	←↰	B6320	**Hexham**	0.5
0.5	Bellingham	↱	minor	**Newcastleton**	24
24.5	B6357 T-junction	↱	B6357	**Bonchester Bridge**	7.5
32	A6088 T-junction	↰	A6088	**Bonchester Bridge**	1
33	Bonchester Bridge	↱	B6357	**Jedburgh**	8.5
41.5	A68 T-junction	↱	A68	**Corbridge**	21.5
63	A68	↱	A68	**Corbridge**	2.5
65.5	A68	↱	B6320	**Bellingham**	7
72.5	Bellingham				

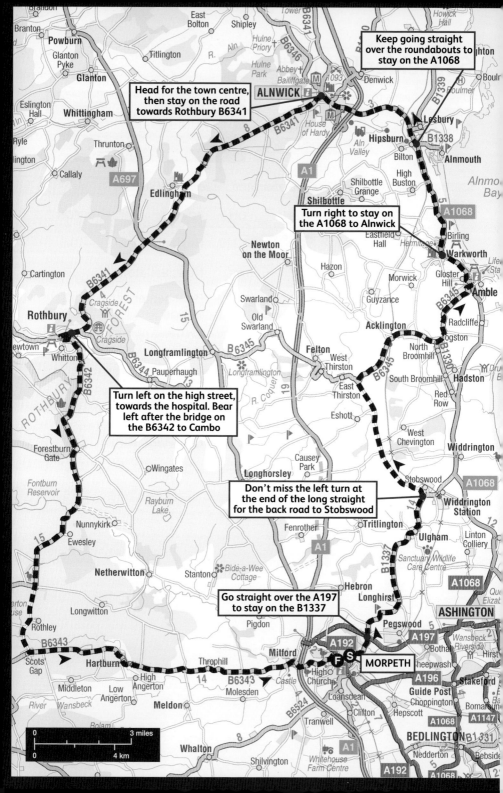

63 Morpeth Rideout

Lots to see along the way on this route, if you fancy stopping at the castles in Warkworth or Alnwick. But with B-roads this good, I'd just keep riding.

FROM	Morpeth
DISTANCE	59 miles
ALLOW	1 hr 35 mins

Starting station: Morrisons, Dark Lane, Morpeth NE61 1ST

MILE	LOCATION	TURN	ON	TO	FOR
0	Morpeth	⊙→	B1337	**Ashington**	6.5
6.5	B1337	↰	minor	**Stobswood**	4
10.5	B6345 T-junction	↱	B6345	**Acklington**	3.5
14	Broomhill	↰	B6345	**Amble**	2.5
16.5	Amble	↰	A1068	**Alnwick**	1
17.5	Warkworth	↱	A1068	**Alnwick**	7.5
24.5	Alnwick	⊙ ⅄	B6346	**Town centre**	12.5
37	Rothbury	↰	B6342	**Hospital**	11
48	Scots Gap	↰	B6343	**Morpeth**	11
59	Morpeth				

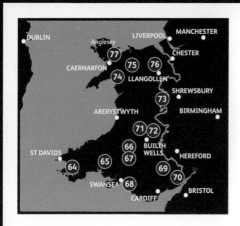

Wales

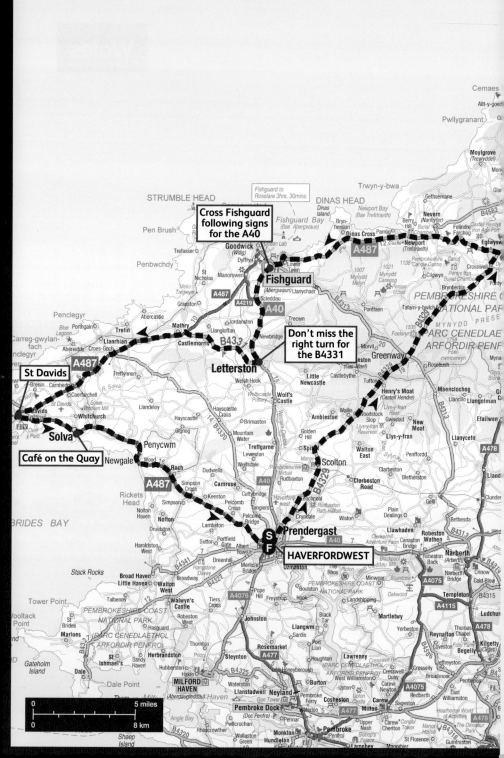

Cross Fishguard following signs for the A40

Don't miss the right turn for the B4331

St Davids

Solva

Café on the Quay

Prendergast

HAVERFORDWEST

64 Wild Haverfordwest

This route is built around one road – the B4329 across the Preseli Mountains – and two great destinations, St Davids and Solva on the run back to Haverfordwest.

FROM	Haverfordwest
DISTANCE	66 miles
ALLOW	1 hr 30 mins

Starting station: Morrisons, Bridge Meadow Lane, Haverfordwest SA61 2EX

MILE	LOCATION	TURN	ON	TO	FOR
0	Haverfordwest	⭦	B4329	**Prendergast**	19
19	Eglwyswrw	↰	A487	**Fishguard**	12
31	Fishguard	⭦	A487	**Haverfordwest (A40)**	0.5
31.5	Fishguard	⭦	A40	**Haverfordwest**	5
36.5	Letterston	↱	B4331	**St Davids (A487)**	4
40.5	A487 T-junction	↰	A487	**St Davids**	9.5
50	St Davids	↰	A487	**Haverfordwest**	16
66	Haverfordwest				

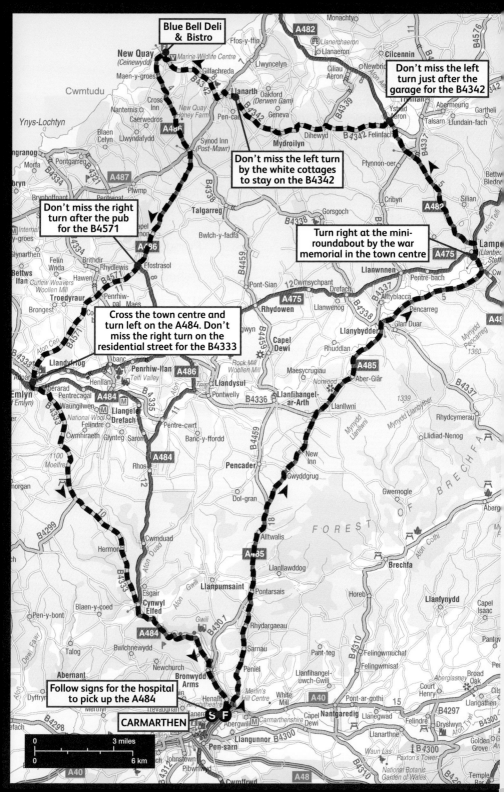

65 Carmarthen Loop

There are so many madly twisty roads between Carmarthen and the coast – and they're usually very quiet. This route strings together a selection of my favourites.

FROM	Carmarthen
DISTANCE	71.5 miles
ALLOW	2 hrs

Starting station: Gulf, Tanerdy Garage, Tanerdy, Carmarthen SA31 2EY

MILE	LOCATION	TURN	ON	TO	FOR
0	Carmarthen	↰ ↤⟳	A484	**Lampeter**	0.5
0.5	Carmarthen	⟳→ ⟳	A485	**Lampeter**	21
21.5	A482 T-junction	↰	A482	**Lampeter**	0.5
22	Lampeter	⟳→	A482	**A482**	6.5
28.5	Felinfach	↰	B4342	**Llanarth**	7
35.5	B4342	↰	B4342	**Llanarth**	0.5
36	Llanarth	↰ ↱	B4342	**New Quay**	3.5
39.5	New Quay	↑	A486	**Llandysul**	4
43.5	A487 (Synod)	⊤↰	A486	**Llandysul**	5
48.5	Ffostrasol	↱	B4571	**Newcastle Emlyn**	6
54.5	Newcastle Emlyn	⟳ ↰	A484	**Carmarthen**	0.5
55	Newcastle Emlyn	↱	B4333	**Cynwyl Elfed**	10
65	Cynwyl Elfed	↱	A484	**Carmarthen**	6.5
71.5	Carmarthen				

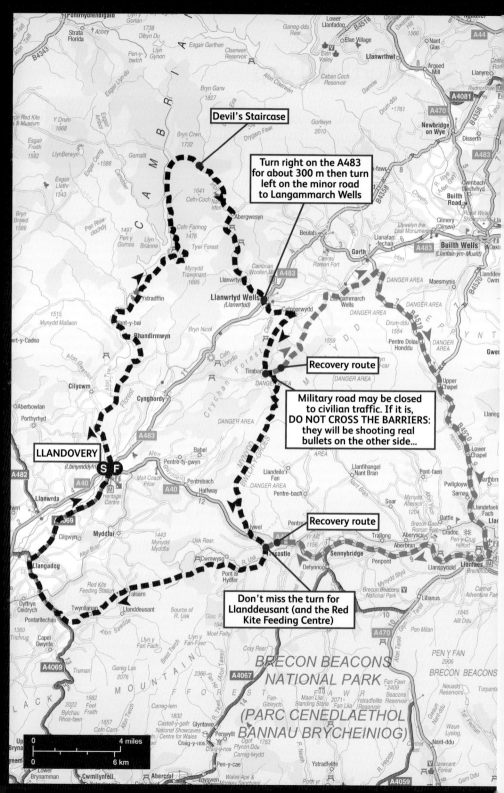

Devil's Staircase

Turn right on the A483 for about 300 m then turn left on the minor road to Langammarch Wells

Recovery route

Military road may be closed to civilian traffic. If it is, DO NOT CROSS THE BARRIERS: they will be shooting real bullets on the other side...

Recovery route

Don't miss the turn for Llanddeusant (and the Red Kite Feeding Centre)

LLANDOVERY
(Llanymddyfri)

BRECON BEACONS NATIONAL PARK
(PARC CENEDLAETHOL BANNAU BRYCHEINIOG)

66 Llandovery Tough Loop

Almost all these roads are narrow, bumpy, with iffy surfaces and a chance of sheep... It's a challenge and I love it, especially on an adventure bike. If live firing closes the road to Llywell, go to Garth and take the B4519.

FROM	Llandovery
DISTANCE	64.5 miles
ALLOW	2 hrs

Starting station: Morris Isaacs, Queensway, Llandovery SA20 0EG

MILE	LOCATION	TURN	ON	TO	FOR
0	Llandovery	↰ ↰	A483	**Builth Wells**	200 m
0	Llandovery	↰	minor	**Cil-y-cwm**	20
20	T-junction	↱	minor	**Abergwesyn**	4.5
24.5	T-junction	↱	minor	**Llanwrtyd Wells**	5
29.5	Llanwrtyd Wells	↱ ↰	minor	**Cefyn Gorwydd**	2
31.5	crossroads	✛	minor	**Tirabad**	3
34.5	Tirabad	↰	minor	**Llywel**	0.5
35	Tirabad	↱	minor	**Llywel**	8.5
43.5	Llywel	↰	A40	**Brecon**	1
44.5	Trecastle	↱	minor	**Llanddeusant**	11
55.5	T-junction	↱	A4069	**Llangadog**	3
58.5	Llangadog	↱	A4069	**Llandovery**	6
64.5	Llandovery				

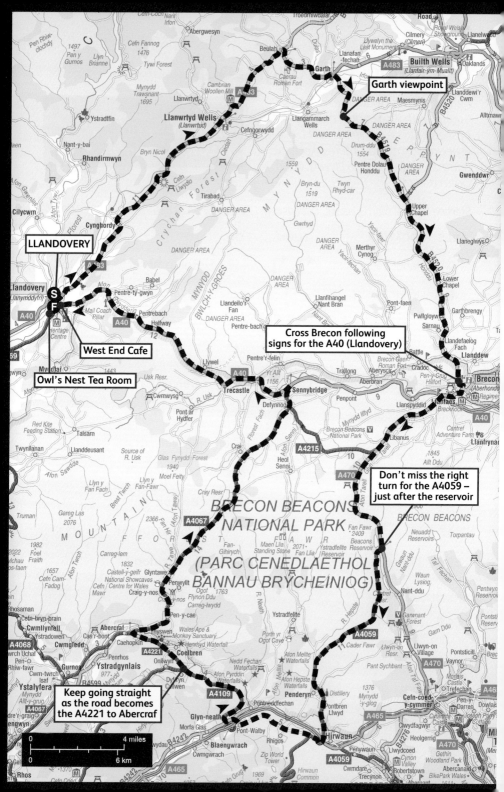

67 Llandovery Long Loop

I've been filling up at Morris Isaacs in Llandovery for as long as I've been riding. This long loop packs in so many brilliant roads. Do stop to appreciate the view from the Garth viewpoint on the B5419.

FROM	Llandovery
DISTANCE	92 miles
ALLOW	2 hrs

Starting station: Morris Isaacs, Queensway, Llandovery SA20 0EG

MILE	LOCATION	TURN	ON	TO	FOR
0	Llandovery	↰ ↰	A483	**Builth Wells**	18
18	Garth	↱	B5419	**Upper Chapel**	7.5
25.5	T-junction	↱	B5420	**Upper Chapel**	9
34.5	Brecon	↱ 🚦↱	B4601	**A40**	1
35.5	A40 roundabout	⊙	A470	**Merthyr Tydfil**	9
44.5	Beacons Reservoir	↱	A4059	**Hirwaun**	9.5
54	Hirwaun	⊙	A4061	**Treherbert**	0.5
54.5	Hirwaun	⊙	minor	**Rhigos Ind Est**	4.5
59	Glyn-neath	🚦↱	A4109	**Seven Sisters**	6.5
65.5	T-junction	↱	A6047	**Pontsenni**	14
79.5	Sennybridge	↰	A40	**Llandovery**	12.5
92	Llandovery				

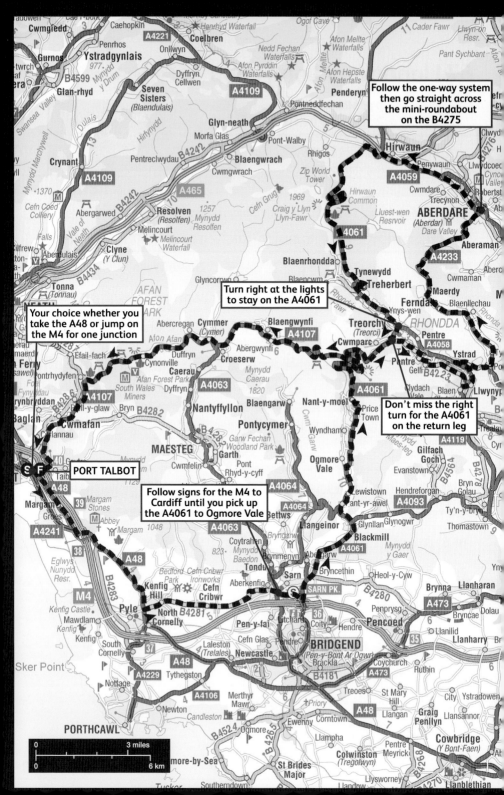

Follow the one-way system then go straight across the mini-roundabout on the B4275

Turn right at the lights to stay on the A4061

Your choice whether you take the A48 or jump on the M4 for one junction

Don't miss the right turn for the A4061 on the return leg

PORT TALBOT

Follow signs for the M4 to Cardiff until you pick up the A4061 to Ogmore Vale

68 Port Talbot Butterfly

This route flits between slow going in the towns and villages of the Valleys to the wide-open spaces between them. It's easily shortened by heading straight back to Port Talbot from the Bwlch viewpoint.

FROM	Port Talbot
DISTANCE	71 miles
ALLOW	2 hr 25 mins

Starting station: Applegreen, 1 Talbot Road, Port Talbot SA13 1HN

MILE	LOCATION	TURN	ON	TO	FOR
0	Port Talbot	↱	A48	**Cardiff**	2.5
2.5	M4 roundabout	←⟳	A48	**Pyle Y Pil**	3.5
6	Pyle	↰	B4281	**Aberkenfig**	4.5
10.5	roundabout	⟳ ←⟳	A4061	**Pontycymer**	14.5
24.5	T-junction	↱	B4223	**Tonypandy**	3
27.5	Tonypandy	←🚦	A4058	**Treorchy**	1
28.5	Ystrad	⟳→	B4512	**Penrhys**	1.5
30	Tylorstown	←⟳	A4233	**Aberdare**	8.5
38.5	Aberdare	⟳	B4275	**Trecynon**	1.5
40	A4059 r'bout	⟳	A4095	**Hirwaun**	1.5
41.5	A465 r'bout	⟳	A465	**Merthyr Tydfil**	0.5
42	A465 r'bout	←⟳ ←⟳	A4061	**Treherbert**	10.5
52.5	Treorchy	↱	A4061	**Ogmore Vale**	3
55.5	Bwlch viewpoint	↱	A4107	**Port Talbot**	15.5
71	Port Talbot				

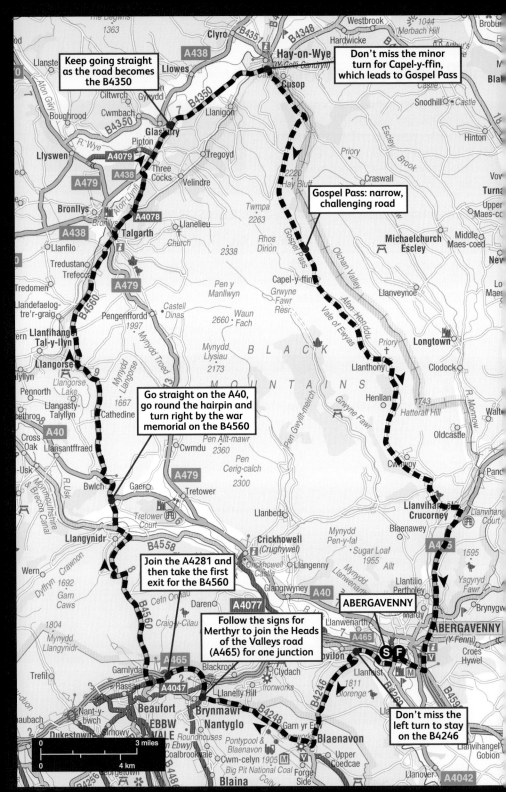

Keep going straight as the road becomes the B4350

Don't miss the minor turn for Capel-y-ffin, which leads to Gospel Pass

Gospel Pass: narrow, challenging road

Go straight on the A40, go round the hairpin and turn right by the war memorial on the B4560

Join the A4281 and then take the first exit for the B4560

Follow the signs for Merthyr to join the Heads of the Valleys road (A465) for one junction

ABERGAVENNY

Don't miss the left turn to stay on the B4246

69 Abergavenny and Gospel Pass

This route features one of my favourite roads in the UK – the B4560. It also includes the highest road in Wales, Gospel Pass. That can be challenging at times, making this a route more suited to confident riders.

FROM	**Abergavenny**
DISTANCE	**60 miles**
ALLOW	**1 hr 40 mins**

Starting station: Waitrose, Merthyr Road, Llanfoist, Abergavenny NP7 9LL

MILE	LOCATION	TURN	ON	TO	FOR
0	Abergavenny		B4246	**Blaenavon**	1.5
1.5	B4246		B4246	**Blaenavon**	3
4.5	Blaenavon		B4248	**Brynmawr**	5
9.5	Brynmawr		A465	**Merthyr Tydfil**	1.5
11	A465		A4281	**Ebbw Vale**	1
12	T-junction		B4560	**Llangynidr**	6
18	T-junction		B4558	**Talybont-on-Usk**	0.5
18.5	Llangynidr		B4560	**Bwlch**	1
19.5	Bwlch		A40	**Brecon**	0.5
20	Bwlch		B4560	**Llangors**	8
28	Talgarth		A4078	**Three Cocks**	2.5
30.5	T-junction		A438	**Hay-on-Wye**	5.5
36	Hay-on-Wye		minor	**Capel-y-ffin**	17.5
53.5	Llanvihangle Crucorney		A465	**Abergavenny**	6.5
60	Abergavenny				

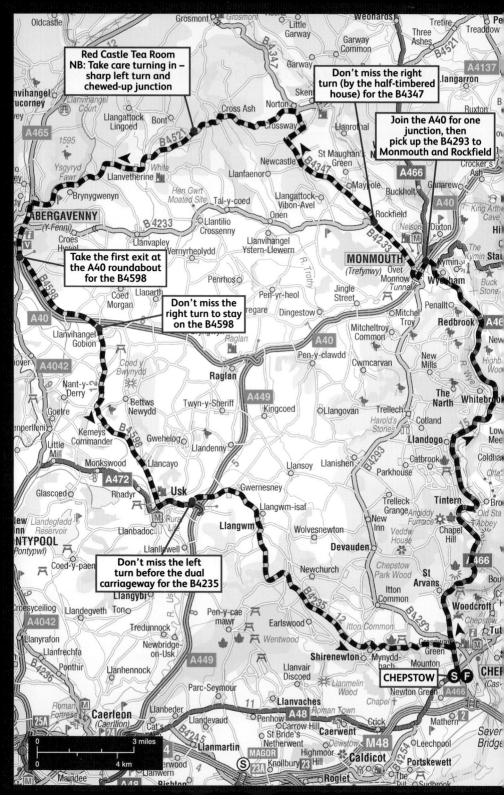

70 Chepstow Rideout

The A466 that hugs the border between England and Wales is a classic bike route – but the brilliant B-roads it links with make this an awesome rideout.

FROM	Chepstow
DISTANCE	60 miles
ALLOW	1 hr 30 mins

Starting station: BP, Newport Road, Chepstow NP16 5YS

MILE	LOCATION	TURN	ON	TO	FOR
0	Chepstow	↰ ⊙→	A466	**Tintern**	16
16	Monmouth	←▮	A40	**Abergavenny**	0.5
16.5	Monmouth	↑ ↱	B4293	**Monmouth**	2.5
19	Rockfield	↑	B4347	**Newcastle**	5.5
24.5	T-junction	↰	B4521	**Abergavenny**	10
34.5	B4521	↱ ↰	A465	**Merthyr Tydfil**	2
36.5	A40 roundabout	←⊙	B4598	**Usk**	3.5
40	B4598	↱	B4598	**Usk**	6
46	Usk	↰	A472	**Newport**	1
47	A472	↰	B4235	**Chepstow**	13
60	Chepstow				

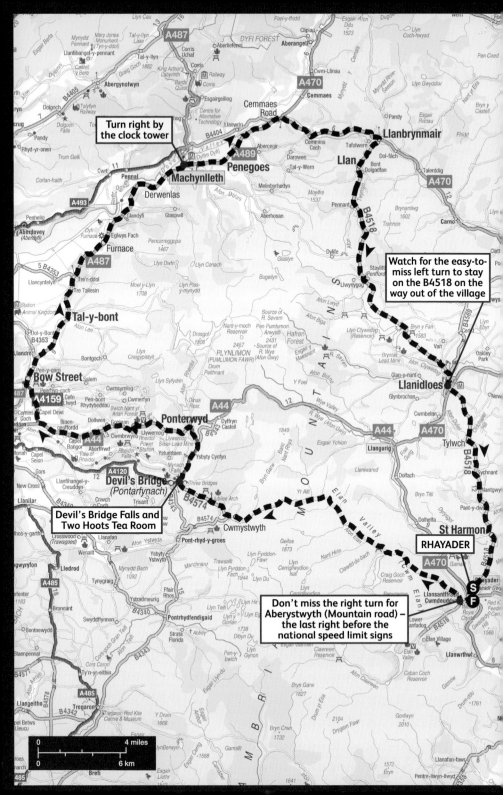

Turn right by the clock tower

Watch for the easy-to-miss left turn to stay on the B4518 on the way out of the village

Devil's Bridge Falls and Two Hoots Tea Room

RHAYADER

Don't miss the right turn for Aberystwyth (Mountain road) – the last right before the national speed limit signs

71 Easy Rhayader

The Elan Valley is a bit of a magnet for adventure bikes, but this relaxed route cuts through to Devil's Bridge on the laid-back mountain road. It's the start of a great ride that suits all kinds of bikes.

FROM	Rhayader
DISTANCE	84.5 miles
ALLOW	2 hrs

Starting station: Texaco, East Street, Rhayader LD6 5EA

MILE	LOCATION	TURN	ON	TO	FOR
0	Rhayader	↱	B4518	**Elan Valley**	0.5
0.5	Rhayader	↱	minor	**Aberystwyth**	18
18.5	The Hafod hotel	↱	A4120	**Ponterwyd**	3
21.5	Ponterwyd	↰	A44	**Aberystwyth**	8.5
30	Lovesgrove r'bout	⬥→	A4159	**Bow Street**	2
32	A487 T-junction	↱	A487	**Machynlleth**	14.5
46.5	Machynlleth	↱	A489	**Newtown**	5.5
52	Cemmaes Road	⬥→	A470	**Llangurig**	6
58	Llanbrynmair	↱	B4518	**Llan**	14.5
72.5	Llanidloes	↱⬥→	B4518	**Town centre**	0.5
73	Llanidloes	↰	B4518	**Tylwch**	11.5
84.5	Rhayader				

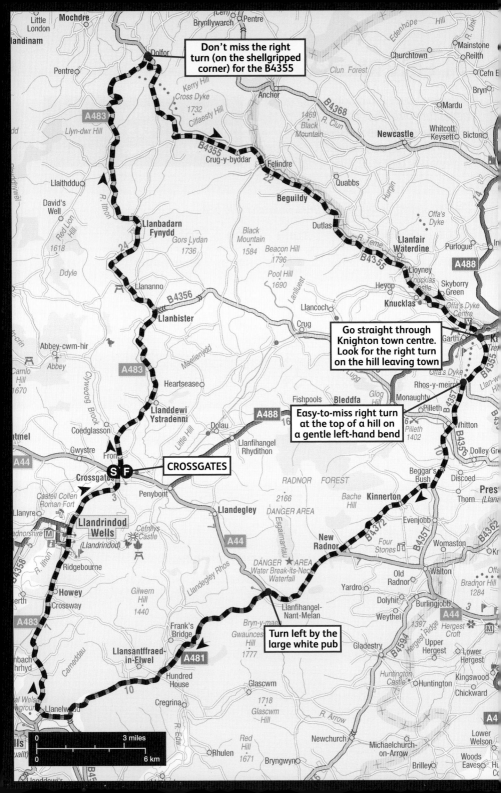

72 Crossgates Classic

With its garage and cafe, Crossgates on the A483 is a classic meeting point for Welsh bikers. Everyone has their own favourite ride here – and this is mine!

FROM	Crossgates
DISTANCE	69 miles
ALLOW	1 hr 30 mins

Starting station: Texaco, Crossgates Service Station, A44, Crossgates LD1 6RE

MILE	LOCATION	TURN	ON	TO	FOR
0	Crossgates		A483	**Newtown**	18.5
18.5	Dolfor		B4355	**Knighton**	17
35.5	Knighton		minor	**Town centre**	0.5
36	Knighton		B4355	**Presteigne**	2
38	B4355		B4357	**Whitton**	4
42	Beggar's Bush		B4372	**Kinnerton**	4
46	New Radnor		A44	**Rhayader**	3
49	A44		A481	**Hundred House**	9.5
58.5	roundabout		A481	**Builth Wells**	0.5
59	Builth Wells		A483	**Llandrindod Wells**	10
69	Crossgates				

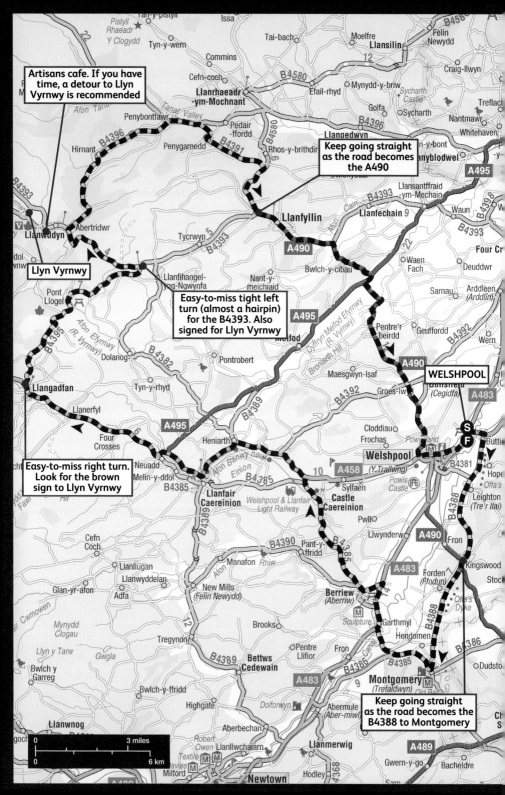

Artisans cafe. If you have time, a detour to Llyn Vyrnwy is recommended

Keep going straight as the road becomes the A490

Llyn Vyrnwy

Easy-to-miss tight left turn (almost a hairpin) for the B4393. Also signed for Llyn Vyrnwy

Easy-to-miss right turn. Look for the brown sign to Llyn Vyrnwy

Keep going straight as the road becomes the B4388 to Montgomery

WELSHPOOL

73 Welshpool Rideout

I really enjoyed putting this route together, getting better acquainted with the excellent B-roads between Lake Vyrnwy and Welshpool. If you have time, add in a lap of the lake.

FROM	Welshpool
DISTANCE	64.5 miles
ALLOW	1 hr 15 mins

Starting station: Texaco, Buttington Cross, Welshpool SY21 8SL

MILE	LOCATION	TURN	ON	TO	FOR
0	Welshpool	↱ ⟳	A458	**Shrewsbury**	0.5
0.5	A458	↱	B4388	**Leighton**	4.5
5	Kingswood	↰	A490	**Chirbury**	3.5
8.5	Montgomery	↱	B4385	**Newtown**	2.5
11	A483 T-junction	↱	A483	**Welshpool**	1.5
12.5	A483	↰	B4390	**Berriew**	1
13.5	Berriew	↱	B4385	**Castel Caereinion**	4.5
18	A458 T-junction	↰	A458	**Dolgellau**	11
29	A458	↱	B4395	**Llwydiarth**	7
36	B4395	↰	B4393	**Llanwddyn**	3.5
39.5	Abertridwr	↱	B4396	**Pen-y-bont Fawr**	5.5
45	Penybontfawr	↱	B4391	**Llanfyllin**	10.5
55.5	A495 T-junction	↰	A495	**Meifod**	0.5
56	A495	↱	A490	**Welshpool**	8.5
64.5	Welshpool				

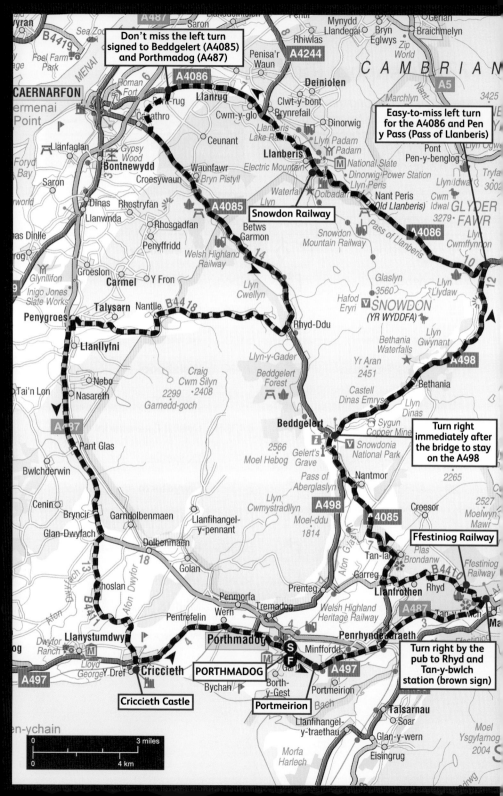

74 Snowdon Rideout

So many fantastic roads in Snowdonia. This ride from Porthmadog links the famous Pass of Llanberis with smaller, more challenging roads like the B4418 to Nantile for a varied and rewarding ride.

FROM	Porthmadog
DISTANCE	66 miles
ALLOW	1 hr 40 mins

Starting station: Shell, High Street, Porthmadog LL49 9NG

MILE	LOCATION	TURN	ON	TO	FOR
0	Porthmadog	↰	A497	**Dolgellau**	2
2	A487 roundabout	⭡	A487	**Dolgellau**	4.5
6.5	Tan-y-bwlch	↰	B4410	**Rhyd**	3.5
10	Garreg	↱	A4085	**Beddgelert**	4.5
14.5	A498 T-junction	↱	A498	**Beddgelert**	1.5
16	Beddgelert	↱	A498	**Capel Curig**	7
23	A498	↰	A4086	**Llanberis**	11.5
34.5	A4086	↰	minor	**Beddgelert**	1.5
36	A4085 r'bout	⭠⭕	A4085	**Beddgelert**	7
43	Rhyd-Ddu	↱	B4418	**Nantile**	7.5
50.5	Penygroes	↰ ⭕⭢	B4418	**Porthmadog**	0.5
51	Penygroes	⭠⭕	A487	**Porthmadog**	6
57	Glan-Dwyfach	↱	B4411	**Criccieth**	4
61	Criccieth	↰	A497	**Porthmadog**	5
66	Porthmadog				

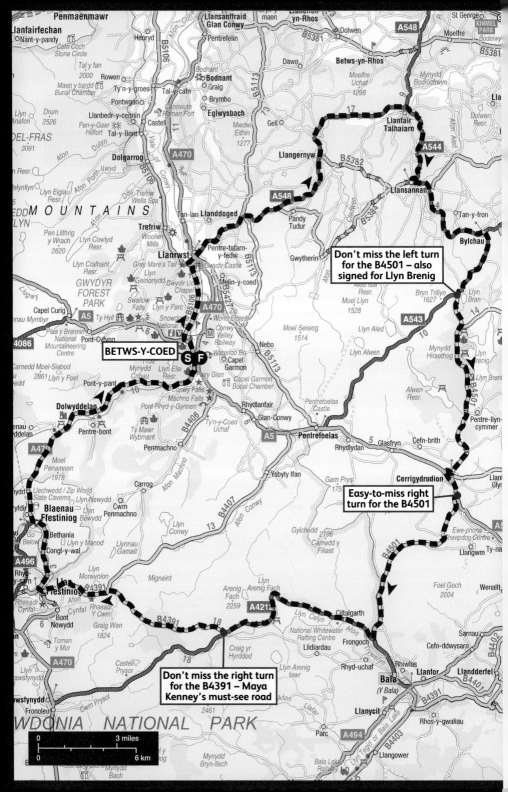

Don't miss the left turn for the B4501 – also signed for Llyn Brenig

Easy-to-miss right turn for the B4501

Don't miss the right turn for the B4391 – Maya Kenney's must-see road

BETWS-Y-COED

75 Betws the Devil You Know…

Tour guide and Welsh-route expert Maja Kenney picked one of my favourites as the must-see road, but stressed it should be ridden in the opposite direction to the one I usually take – which led to this great route.

FROM	Betws-y-Coed
DISTANCE	72.5 miles
ALLOW	1 hr 40 mins

Starting station: Shell, Waterloo Bridge, Betws-y-Coed LL24 0AR

MILE	LOCATION	TURN	ON	TO	FOR
0	Betws-y-Coed	↰	A5	**Bangor**	0.5
0.5	Betws-y-Coed	↱	B5106	**Trefriw**	3.5
4	T-junction	↱	B5106	**Llanrwst**	0.5
4.5	Llanrwst	↰ ↱	A458	**Abergele**	11.5
16	Llanfair Talhaiarn	↱	A544	**Llansannan**	8
24	Bylchau	↱	A543	**Pentrefoelas**	3
27	A543	↰	B4501	**Cerrigydrudion**	7.5
34.5	Cerrigydrudion	↱ ↰	A5	**Llangollen**	1
35.5	A5	↱	B4501	**Bala**	7.5
43	A4212 T-junction	↱	A4212	**Trawsfynydd**	7
50	A4212	↱	B4391	**Ffestiniog**	8
58	A470 T-junction	↱	A470	**Betws-y-Coed**	3.5
61.5	Blaenau Ffestiniog	⭥	A470	**Betws-y-Coed**	11
72.5	Betws-y-Coed				

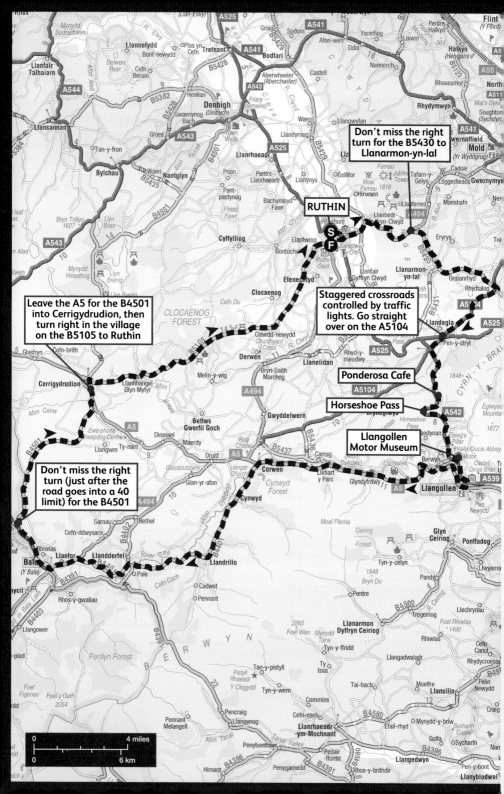

76 Ruthin Tumble

Sadly, much of this corner of Wales is blighted by 50 mph limits – but there is still some great riding and it's amazingly scenic. It's not compulsory to stop at the Ponderosa Cafe on Horseshoe Pass, but it is recommended.

FROM	Ruthin
DISTANCE	68.5 miles
ALLOW	1 hr 35 mins

Starting station: BP, Park Road, Ruthin LL15 1NB

MILE	LOCATION	TURN	ON	TO	FOR
0	Ruthin	↱	A494	**Mold**	4
4	A494	↱	B5430	**Llanarmon**	6
10	A5104 X-roads	┼	A5104	**Llandegla**	3
13	A525	🚦↰	A5104	**Corwen**	1
14	roundabout	←⟳	A542	**Llangollen**	7.5
21.5	Llangollen	↱ 🚦	A5	**Betws-y-Coed**	10.5
32	Corwen	↰	B4401	**Cynwyd**	11
43	A494 T-junction	↰	A494	**Bala**	1
44	Bala	↱	A4212	**Trawsfynydd**	2.5
46.5	A4212	↱	B4501	**Cerrigydrudion**	7.5
54	A5 T-junction	↰	A5	**Betws-y-Coed**	0.5
54.5	A5	⋏	B4501	**Cerrigydrudion**	0.5
55	Cerrigydrudion	↱	B5105	**Ruthin**	13.5
68.5	Ruthin				

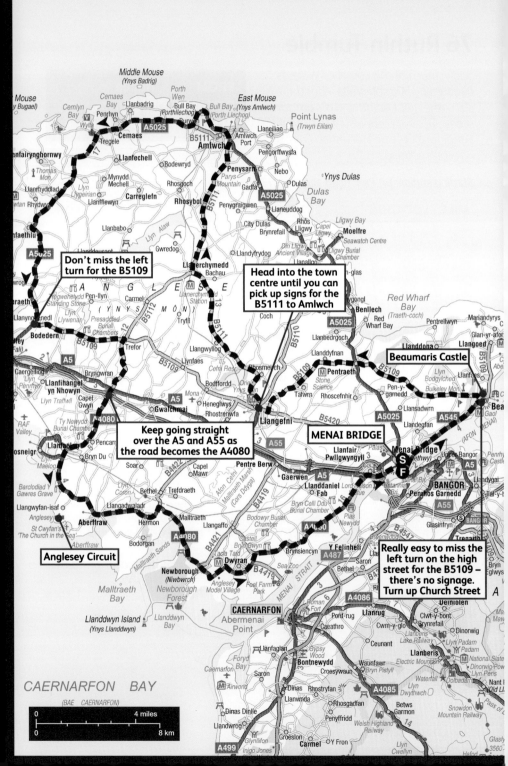

Don't miss the left turn for the B5109

Head into the town centre until you can pick up signs for the B5111 to Amlwch

Beaumaris Castle

MENAI BRIDGE

Keep going straight over the A5 and A55 as the road becomes the A4080

Anglesey Circuit

Really easy to miss the left turn on the high street for the B5109 – there's no signage. Turn up Church Street

77 Anglesey Loop

This gentle lap of Anglesey is a whole lot more laid-back than a lap of the island's race track – it's perfectly suited to a relaxed ride, maybe with a sightseeing stop at Beaumaris Castle.

FROM	Menai Bridge
DISTANCE	72.5 miles
ALLOW	1 hr 55 mins

Starting station: Shell, Mona Road, Menai Bridge LL59 5EB

MILE	LOCATION	TURN	ON	TO	FOR
0	Menai Bridge		A545	**Beaumaris**	4.5
4.5	Beaumaris		B5109	**Church Street**	5.5
10	Pentraeth		B5109	**Llangefni**	4
14	Llangefni		B5420	**Town centre**	0.5
14.5	Llangefni		B5110	**Benllech**	0.5
15	Llangefni		B5111	**Amlwch**	6.5
21.5	Llanerchymedd		B5111	**Rhosybol**	6
27.5	Amlwch		A5025	**Amlwch**	15.5
43	Llanynghenedl		B5109	**Bodedern**	4
47	Trefor		B5112	**Rhosneigr (A5)**	11.5
58.5	T-junction		A4080	**Newborough**	12
70.5	A5 T-junction		A5	**Menai Bridge**	2
72.5	Menai Bridge				

THURSO

92
ULLAPOOL

ELGIN
PORTREE   INVERNESS   90
                93 89

PORTREE

ABERDEEN
91

FORT WILLIAM

88

OBAN 87   86 PERTH

85 STIRLING

83   84   EDINBURGH
     GLASGOW   81

AYR   79   82

80 HAWICK   ALNWICK

STRANRAER   78

CARLISLE

Scotland

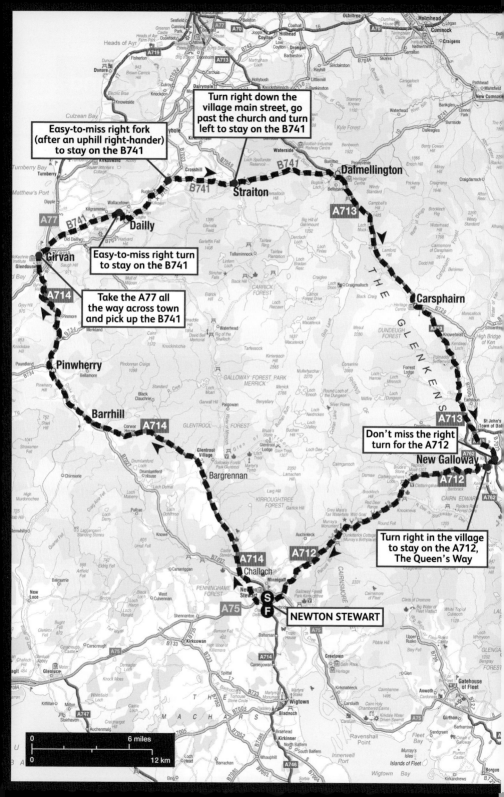

Turn right down the village main street, go past the church and turn left to stay on the B741

Easy-to-miss right fork (after an uphill right-hander) to stay on the B741

Easy-to-miss right turn to stay on the B741

Take the A77 all the way across town and pick up the B741

Don't miss the right turn for the A712

Turn right in the village to stay on the A712, The Queen's Way

NEWTON STEWART

78 Newton Stewart Square

This longer ride cuts through the wide-open spaces of Galloway Forest Park, heading to the coast at Girvan before looping back inland to pick up the epic A713 and the beautiful A712, The Queen's Way.

FROM	Newton Stewart
DISTANCE	93 miles
ALLOW	2 hrs

Starting station: BP, Wigtown Road, Newton Stewart DG8 6JZ

MILE	LOCATION	TURN	ON	TO	FOR
0	Newton Stewart	↱ ⟳→	A75	**Stranraer**	1
1	A75	↱	minor	**Girvan (A714)**	1.5
2.5	A714 T-junction	↰	A714	**Girvan**	27
29.5	Girvan	⟳	A77	**Ayr**	2
31.5	Girvan	↱	B741	**Dailly**	5
36.5	B741	↱	B741	**Dailly**	1
37.5	Dailly	↰	B741	**Straiton**	4
41.5	B741	↑	B741	**Straiton**	4
45.5	Straiton	↱ ↰	B741	**Dalmellington**	6.5
52	A713 crossroads	┼→	A713	**Dumfries**	21.5
73.5	A713	↱	A712	**New Galloway**	1
74.5	New Galloway	↱	A712	**Newton Stewart**	17
91.5	A75 T-junction	↱	A75	**Stranraer**	1.5
93	Newton Stewart				

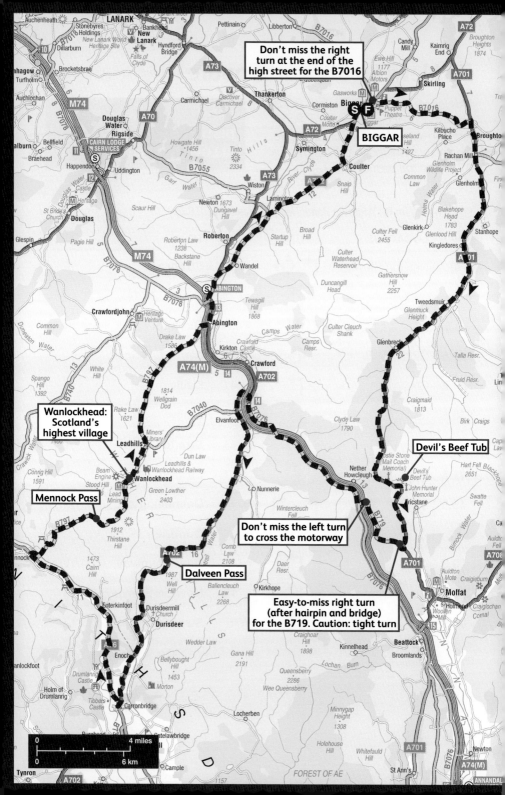

79 Biggar and Better

So many great roads through the Borders in this route, including the Dalveen and Mennock Passes – not to mention the epic A701 past the Devil's Beef Tub.

FROM	Biggar
DISTANCE	88 miles
ALLOW	1 hr 50 mins

Starting station: BP, Coulter Road, Biggar ML12 6EP

MILE	LOCATION	TURN	ON	TO	FOR
0	Biggar	↱ ↱	B7016	**Broughton**	5.5
5.5	Broughton	↱	A701	**Moffat**	20.5
26	A701	↱	B719	**B719**	3
29	B719	↰ ↱	B7076	**Glasgow**	8
37	A702 roundabout	↰⟲	A702	**Elvanfoot**	16
53	Carronbridge	↱	A76	**Kilmarnock**	8.5
61.5	A75	↱	B796	**Abington**	14.5
76	A702 T-junction	↰	A702	**Abington**	1
77	A74(M) r'bout	⟲↗	A702	**Lanark**	11
88	Biggar				

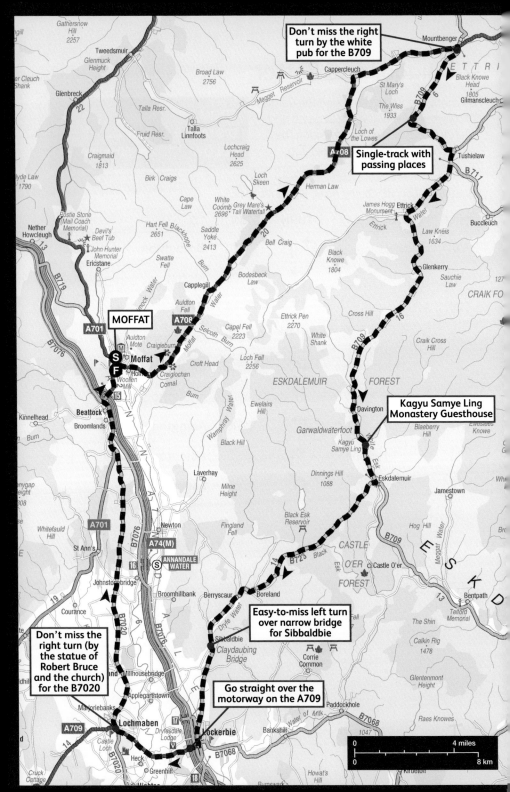

80 Moffat Little Loop

I'm a regular visitor to the Buccleuch Arms Hotel in Moffat, where my friend Dave plots routes for biking guests. This route wouldn't keep you busy all day... so if you want a longer one, you'll need to stay at the hotel and ask Dave!

FROM	Moffat
DISTANCE	76 miles
ALLOW	1 hr 30 mins

Starting station: Esso, Benmar Garage, Church Gate, Moffat DG10 9EL

MILE	LOCATION	TURN	ON	TO	FOR
0	Moffat	↱ ↱	A708	**Selkirk**	21.5
21.5	A708	↱	B709	**Langholm**	6
27.5	B709 T-junction	↱	B709	**Langholm**	15.5
43	Eskdalemuir	↱	B723	**Lockerbie**	10
53	B723	↰	B723	**Sibbaldbie**	4
57	Lockerbie	←◇ ▯↦	A709	**Lochmaben**	4
61	Lochmaben	⋎	B7020	**Templand**	11
72	A701 T-junction	↱	A701	**A74(M)**	2
74	A74(M) r'bout	⊙↰	A701	**Moffat**	2
76	Moffat				

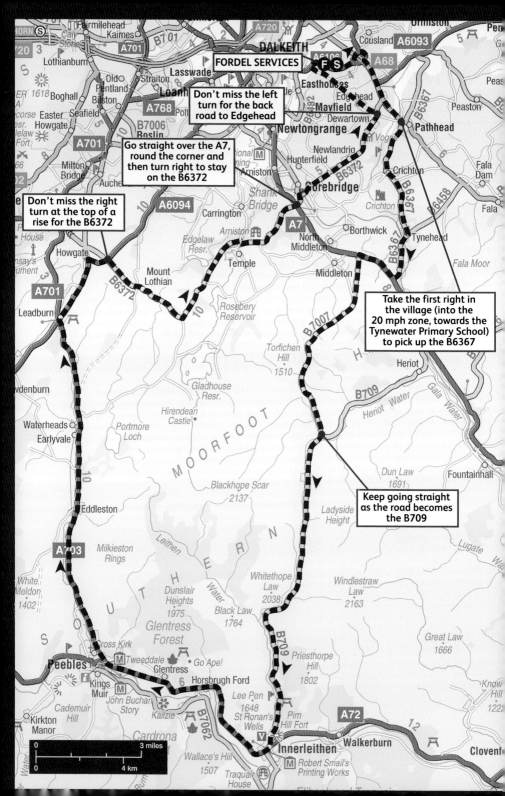

FORDEL SERVICES

Don't miss the left turn for the back road to Edgehead

Go straight over the A7, round the corner and then turn right to stay on the B6372

Don't miss the right turn at the top of a rise for the B6372

Take the first right in the village (into the 20 mph zone, towards the Tynewater Primary School) to pick up the B6367

Keep going straight as the road becomes the B709

81 Dalkeith Rideout

This route actually starts just outside Dalkeith, at the Fordel Services. It's a lovely mix of roads: some narrow, some broad and flowing, showing how much wild countryside there is on Edinburgh's doorstep.

FROM	Dalkeith (Fordel)
DISTANCE	58 miles
ALLOW	1 hr 25 mins

Starting station: Esso, Fordel Services, Lauder Road, Dalkeith EH22 2PH

MILE	LOCATION	TURN	ON	TO	FOR
0	Dalkeith (Fordel)	↰	A6106	**Jedburgh**	1
1	A6106	↰	A68	**Jedburgh**	2.5
3.5	Pathhead	↱	B6367	**Crichton**	1.5
5	Crichton	↰↱	B6367	**Tynehead**	2
7	Tynehead	↱	B6367	**Galashiels**	1
8	A7 T-junction	↱	A7	**Edinburgh**	1.5
9.5	A7	↰	B7007	**Innerleithen**	15.5
25	Innerleithen	↱	A72	**High Street**	6
31	Peebles	⊙→	A703	**Edinburgh**	10
41	Leadburn X-roads	↱	A6094	**Bonnyrigg**	2
43	Howgate	⊙→	A6094	**Bonnyrigg**	0.5
43.5	A6094	↱	B6372	**Gladhouse**	8
51.5	Gorebridge	↱	B6372	**Pathhead**	3.5
55	B6372	↰	minor	**Edgehead**	2.5
57.5	A6106 T-junction	↱	A6106	**Jedburgh**	0.5
58	Dalkeith (Fordel)				

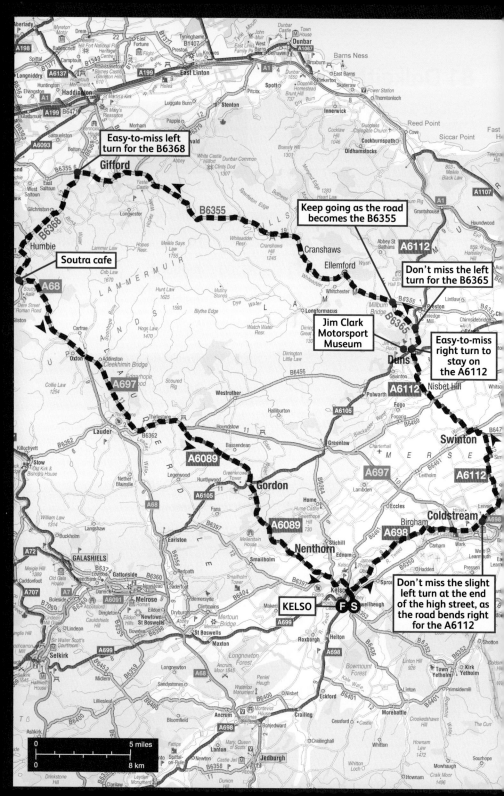

82 Kelso Corners

Easily adapted for Edinburgh riders (just start on the A68 through Pathhead), this route is built around one of my favourite roads in southern Scotland: the B6355 that soars over the moors, past the Whiteadder Reservoir.

FROM	Kelso
DISTANCE	80.5 miles
ALLOW	1 hr 45 mins

Starting station: Sainsbury's, Pinnaclehill Industrial Estate, Kelso TD5 8DW

MILE	LOCATION	TURN	ON	TO	FOR
0	Kelso	⟡→ ⟡→	A698	**Coldstream**	8
8	A697 T-juntion	↱	A698	**Coldstream**	1.5
9.5	Coldstream	↱	A6112	**Duns**	6.5
16	Swinton	↱	A6112	**Duns**	6
22	Duns	↱	A6112	**Preston**	1
23	A6112	⋏	B6365	**Abbey St Bathans**	22
45	B6355	↰	B6368	**Petersmuir**	7.5
52.5	A68 T-junction	↰	A68	**Jedburgh**	6
58.5	Carfraemill r'bout	←⟡	A697	**Coldstream**	7.5
66	A697	↱	A6089	**Gordon**	14.5
80.5	Kelso				

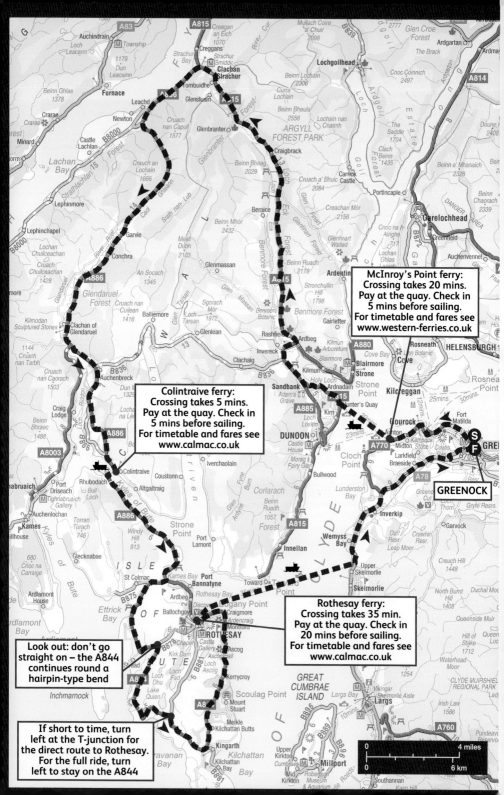

McInroy's Point ferry:
Crossing takes 20 mins.
Pay at the quay. Check in
5 mins before sailing.
For timetable and fares see
www.western-ferries.co.uk

Colintraive ferry:
Crossing takes 5 mins.
Pay at the quay. Check in
5 mins before sailing.
For timetable and fares see
www.calmac.co.uk

Rothesay ferry:
Crossing takes 35 min.
Pay at the quay. Check in
20 mins before sailing.
For timetable and fares see
www.calmac.co.uk

**Look out: don't go
straight on – the A844
continues round a
hairpin-type bend**

**If short to time, turn
left at the T-junction for
the direct route to Rothesay.
For the full ride, turn
left to stay on the A844**

83 Afternoon Island Hopper

This route takes a bit longer than most in this book, but it's worth it for the sheer joy of the roads – and the contrast to suburban Glasgow. Plus the ferries really make it feel like a holiday.

FROM	Greenock
DISTANCE	78 miles
ALLOW	3 hrs 20 mins

Starting station: Tesco, Dalrymple Street, Greenock PA15 1LE

MILE	LOCATION	TURN	ON	TO	FOR
0	Greenock	↱ ↱	A770	**Gourock**	4.5
4.5	McInroy's Point	⛴		**Hunter's Quay**	-
4.5	Hunter's Quay	↱	A815	**Sandbank**	2
6.5	Sandbank	↱	A815	**Glasgow (A82)**	16
22.5	Strachur	↰	A886	**Glendaruel**	21.5
44	Colintraive	⛴		**Rhubodach**	-
44	Rhubodach	↑	A886	**Rothesay**	5.5
49.5	A886	↱	A844	**Ettrick Bay**	10
59.5	T-junction	↱	A844	**Rothesay (10)**	10
69.5	Rothesay	⛴		**Wemyss Bay**	-
69.5	Wemyss Bay	↰	A78	**Glasgow**	8.5
78	Greenock				

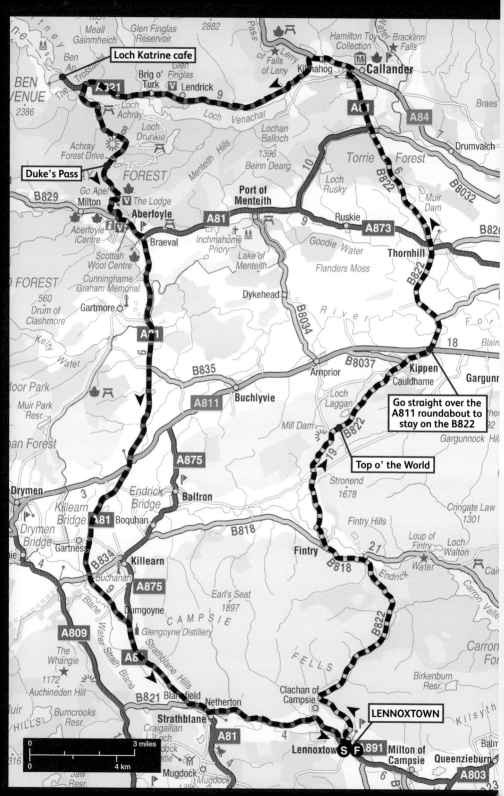

84 Top o' the World

Does any other city have such good riding so close to it as Glasgow does? This laid-back Lennoxtown loop heads over the Crow Road and the Top o' the World, to cut through the Trossachs on the Duke's Pass. Brilliant!

FROM	Lennoxtown
DISTANCE	60 miles
ALLOW	1 hr 25 mins

Starting station: Lennox Service Station, Main Street, Lennoxtown, Glasgow G66 7HA

MILE	LOCATION	TURN	ON	TO	FOR
0	Lennoxtown	↱ ↱	B822	**Fintry**	8
8	Fintry	↱	B822	**Kippen**	11
19	Thornhill	↑ ↱	B822	**Callander**	6
25	Callander	↰	A84	**Crianlarich**	1
26	Kilmahog	↰	A821	**Aberfoyle**	14
40	Aberfoyle	⟲→	A81	**Glasgow**	15.5
55.5	Strathblane	←⟲	A891	**Campsie Glen**	4.5
60	Lennoxtown				

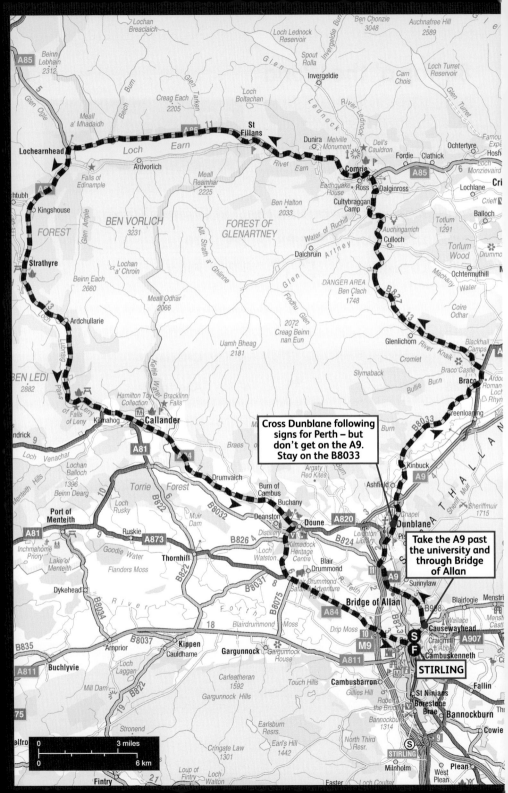

Cross Dunblane following signs for Perth – but don't get on the A9. Stay on the B8033

Take the A9 past the university and through Bridge of Allan

STIRLING

85 Simple Stirling

From Stirling, one good road can lead to another, then another, and another... until you look down and you've done 150 miles, it's four hours later and you're still miles from home. So here's a short, simple alternative.

FROM	Stirling
DISTANCE	65.5 miles
ALLOW	1 hr 40 mins

Starting station: Tesco, Wallace Street, Stirling FK8 1NP

MILE	LOCATION	TURN	ON	TO	FOR
0	Stirling	← ⟡ →	A9	**Bridge of Allan**	4.5
4.5	M9/A9 r'bout	⟳	B8033	**Dunblane**	8.5
13	Braco	←	A822	**Crieff**	0.5
13.5	A822	←	B827	**Comrie**	10.5
24	Comrie	←	A85	**Crianlarich**	12.5
36.5	Lochearnhead	←	A84	**Callander**	29
65.5	Stirling				

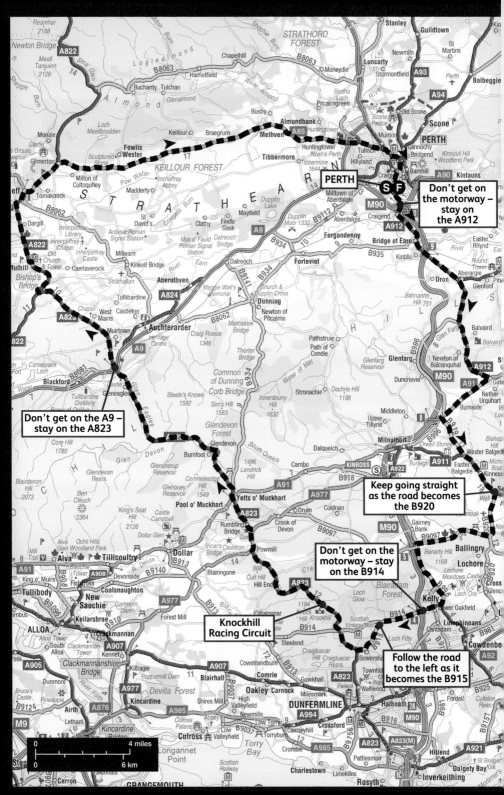

Don't get on the motorway – stay on the A912

Don't get on the A9 – stay on the A823

Keep going straight as the road becomes the B920

Don't get on the motorway – stay on the B914

Knockhill Racing Circuit

Follow the road to the left as it becomes the B915

86 Perth Rideout

For a country with so many great roads, the A9 and M90 rather let the side down... so this route avoids them, taking the twisty, scenic way to reach the A823 that runs past Knockhill, the home of Scottish bike racing.

FROM	Perth
DISTANCE	77 miles
ALLOW	2 hrs

Starting station: Esso, Edinburgh Road, Perth PH2 8DX

MILE	LOCATION	TURN	ON	TO	FOR
0	Perth	↰ ↻	A912	**Bridge of Earn**	10
10	Gateside	↱	A91	**Edinburgh**	3
13	A91	↰	B919	**Scotlandwell**	2
15	Balgedie Toll	↰	A911	**Glenrothes**	3.5
18.5	B920 T-junction	↱ ↱	B9097	**Kinross**	3.5
22	B996 T-junction	↰	B996	**Cowdenbeath**	3
25	Kelty	↱	B914	**Kelty**	4.5
29.5	A823 T-junction	↱	A823	**Crieff**	7.5
37	Powmill	↱	A977	**Kinross**	0.5
37.5	Powmill	↰	A823	**Crieff**	2
39.5	A91 junction	↱ ↻	A823	**Crieff**	13.5
53	A822 T-junction	↱	A822	**Crieff**	5
58	Crieff	↱ ↑	A85	**Perth**	19
77	Perth				

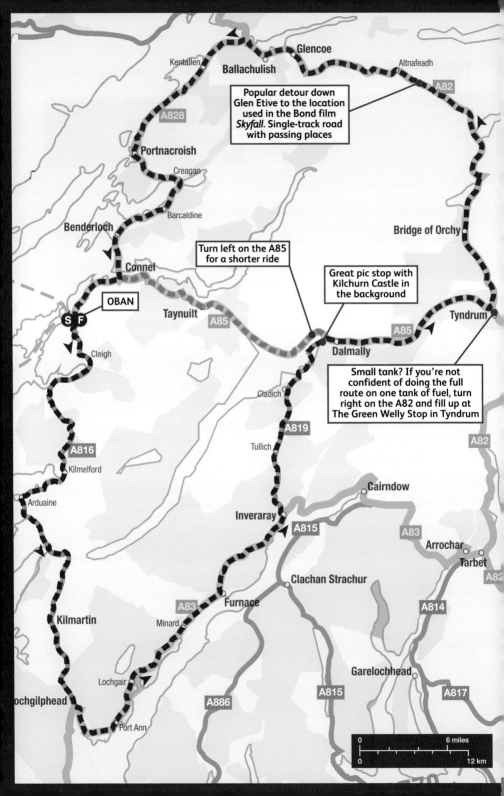

87 Obvious Oban

This is a slightly longer route than most in this book – easily shortened by cutting out Glen Coe. But if you're heading to Oban on holiday, this relaxed ride presents the best views of one of Scotland's finest landscapes.

FROM	Oban
DISTANCE	152 miles
ALLOW	3 hrs

Starting station: Gleaner, Soroba Road, Oban PA34 4HY

MILE	LOCATION	TURN	ON	TO	FOR
0	Oban	↰	A816	**Campbeltown**	36
36	Lochgilphead	↔⟲	A83	**Glasgow**	25
61	Inveraray	↰	A819	**Oban**	14.5
75.5	A85 T-junction	↱	A85	**Crianlarich**	12.5
88	Tyndrum	↰	A82	**Fort William**	33
121	Ballachulish	⟲→	A828	**Oban**	31
152	Oban				

The full-day tourist trip

Take the standard route for 121 miles then go straight over the Ballachulish roundabout on the A82 to Fort William. Fill up at the Gleaner in Onich and then, three miles later, turn left to take the Corran ferry. Arrive at Ardgour and turn left on the A861. After 12.5 miles turn left on the A884 to Lochaline and take the Mull ferry. There's only one road from the quay in Fishnish: at the end of it, turn left on the A849 to Craignure, 4.5 miles away. Take the ferry from there to return to Oban.

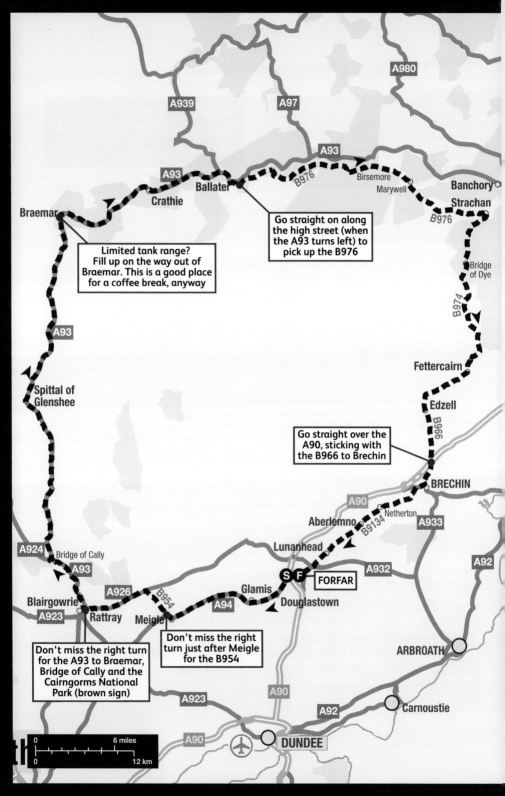

88 Forfar from the Madding Crowd

It's hard to have a short ride that involves going through Glenshee... but it's definitely worth the extra time. This route also uses the narrow but wonderful B974 – an unsung hero of a road.

FROM	Forfar
DISTANCE	128 miles
ALLOW	2 hrs 40 mins

Starting station: Shell, Silvie Way, Orchardbank Business Park, Forfar DD8 1BF

MILE	LOCATION	TURN	ON	TO	FOR
0	Forfar	⬦→	A94	**Coupar Angus**	11
11	A94	↱	B954	**Alyth**	2.5
13.5	A926 roundabout	←⬦	A926	**Blairgowrie**	5
18.5	Blairgowrie	↱	A93	**Braemar**	50
68.5	Ballater	↑ ↰	B976	**Banchory**	21.5
90	Strachan	↱	B974	**Fettercairn**	14
104	Fettercairn	⬦ ↑	B966	**Edzell**	11
115	Brechin	←⬦ ⬦→	A935	**Forfar**	1
116	Brechin	↰	B9134	**Aberlemno**	12
128	Forfar				

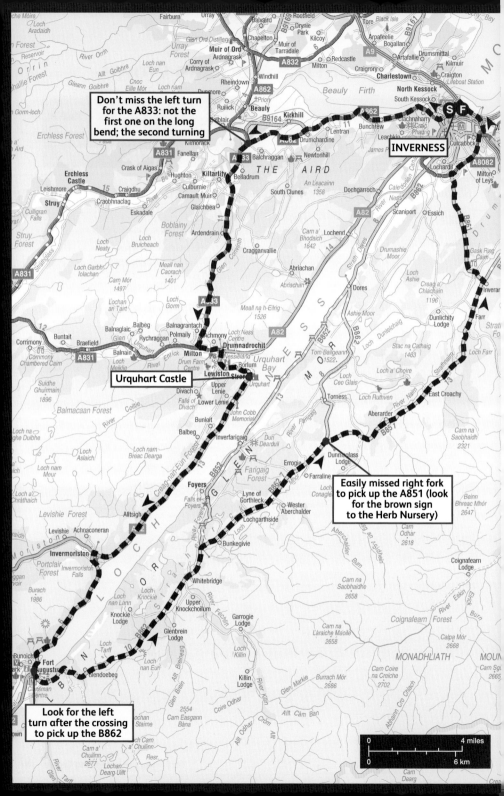

89 Inverness Loop

This lap of Loch Ness aims to minimize the time spent on the often-busy A82 by using entertaining back roads.

FROM	Inverness
DISTANCE	78 miles
ALLOW	1 hr 40 mins

Starting station: BP, 22–24 Longman Road, Inverness IV1 1RY

MILE	LOCATION	TURN	ON	TO	FOR
0	Inverness	↰ ⟳	A82	**Fort William**	0.5
0.5	Inverness	⟳ ⟳	A862	**Beauly**	9.5
10	A862	↰	A833	**Kiltarlity**	10
20	A831 T-junction	↰	A831	**Drumnadrochit**	1
21	Drumnadrochit	↱	A82	**Fort William**	19
40	Fort Augustus	↰	B862	**Whitebridge**	17.5
57.5	B862	↑	B851	**Daviot**	11
68.5	Inverarnie	↰	B861	**Inverness**	9.5
78	Inverness				

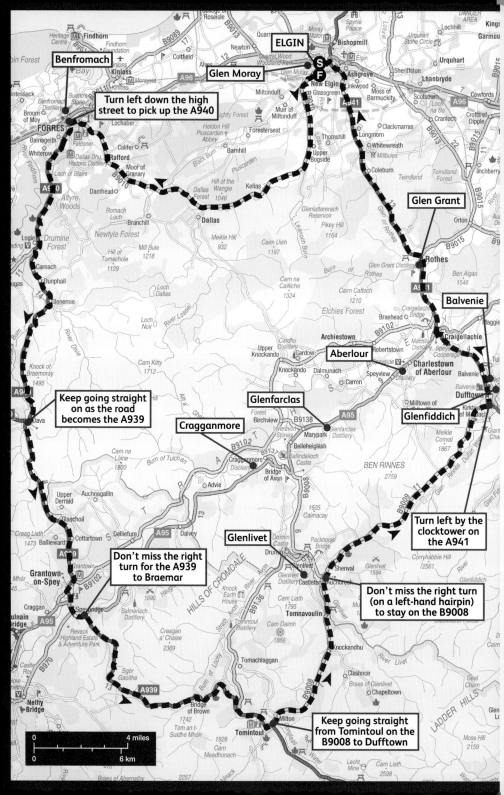

Benfromach

Findhorn

ELGIN

Glen Moray

Turn left down the high
street to pick up the A940

Glen Grant

Balvenie

Aberlour

Glenfarclas

Glenfiddich

Cragganmore

Keep going straight
on as the road
becomes the A939

Turn left by the
clocktower on
the A941

Don't miss the right
turn for the A939
to Braemar

Glenlivet

Don't miss the right turn
(on a left-hand hairpin)
to stay on the B9008

Keep going straight
from Tomintoul on the
B9008 to Dufftown

| 0 | 4 miles |
| 0 | 6 km |

90 Elgin Marvels

This route through the heart of Speyside passes many of the great distilleries – but it's the riding that will really go to your head. Of all the great roads in the area, I've boiled the route down to 90 miles of undiluted pleasure.

FROM	Elgin
DISTANCE	90 miles
ALLOW	2 hrs

Starting station: Esso, West Road, Elgin IV30 1SA

MILE	LOCATION	TURN	ON	TO	FOR
0	Elgin		B9010	**Dallas**	17
17	Forres		B9011	**High Street**	0.5
17.5	Forres		A940	**Grantown-on-Spey**	22
39.5	Grantown-on-Spey		A95	**Elgin**	0.5
40	A95 roundabout		A95	**Elgin**	1
41	A95		A939	**Braemar**	12.5
53.5	Tomintoul		A939	**Braemar**	0.5
54	Tomintoul		B9008	**Dufftown**	7.5
61.5	B9008		B9008	**Dufftown**	10.5
72	Dufftown		A941	**Craigellachie**	4.5
76.5	A95 T-junction		A95	**Elgin (A941)**	13.5
90	Elgin				

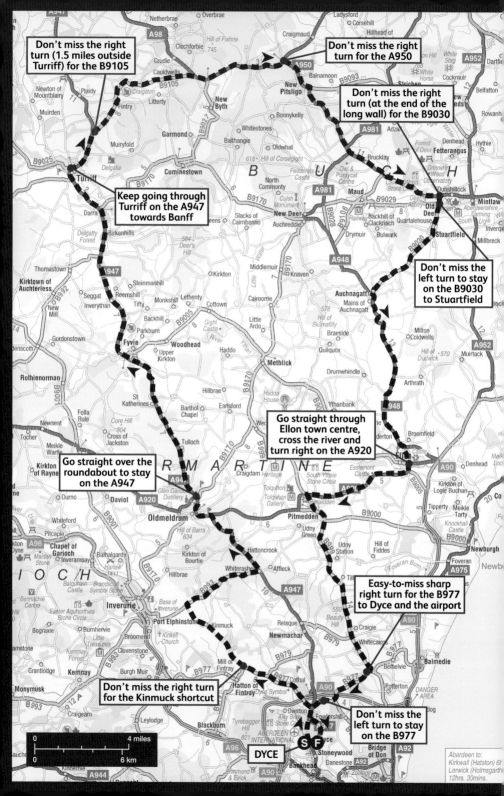

91 Dyce and Easy

While the land around Aberdeen is generally much flatter than the nearby Cairngorms, there's still some lovely riding to be found.

FROM	Dyce
DISTANCE	86.5 miles
ALLOW	2 hrs 5 mins

Starting station: BP, Wellheads Road, Dyce, Aberdeen AB21 7HG

MILE	LOCATION	TURN	ON	TO	FOR
0	Dyce	← ⊙ →	minor	**Airport**	2
2	Dyce	←	B977	**Hatton of Fintray**	3.5
5.5	B977	→	minor	**Kinmuck**	3.5
9	B993 T-junction	→	B993	**Whiterashes**	4
13	Whiterashes	←	A947	**Hattoncrook**	22
35	A947	→	B9105	**Fraserburgh**	6
41	A98 T-junction	→	A98	**Fraserburgh**	4
45	A98	→	A950	**New Pitsligo**	9.5
54.5	A950	→	B9030	**Auchnagatt**	5.5
60	Auchnagatt	←	A948	**Ellon**	7
67	A948	→	minor	**Ellon**	1
68	Ellon	→	A920	**Oldmeldrum**	4.5
72.5	crossroads	← →	B999	**Pitmedden**	8.5
81	B999	→	B977	**Dyce**	2
83	B977	←	B977	**Dyce**	3.5
86.5	Dyce				

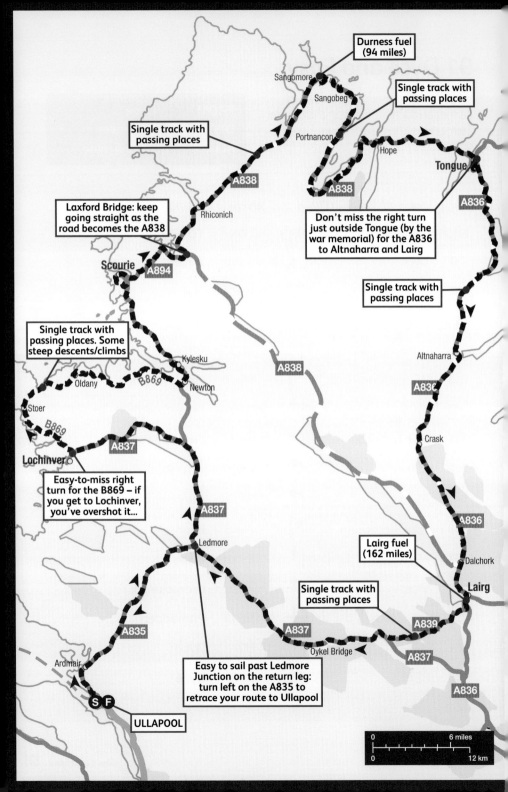

92 Ullapool Balloon

Less of a ride for locals and more of a short, relaxed daytrip ride for visitors to Ullapool (once voted Scotland's most romantic town). Ideal for anyone who doesn't want to carry on along the full North Coast 500 route.

FROM	Ullapool
DISTANCE	206 miles
ALLOW	4 hrs

Starting station: Loch Broom Filling Station, Garve Road, Ullapool IV26 2SY

MILE	LOCATION	TURN	ON	TO	FOR
0	Ullapool	↱	A835	**Kylesku**	18
18	Ledmore Junction	↰	A837	**Lochinver**	17
35	A837	↱	B869	**Achmelvich**	22
57	A894 T-junction	↰	A894	**Kylesku**	67
124	after Tongue	↱	A836	**Altnaharra**	38
162	Lairg	↱	A839	**Ullapool (A837)**	8
170	A837 T-junction	↱	A837	**Lochinver**	18
188	Ledmore Junction	↰	A835	**Ullapool**	18
206	Ullapool				

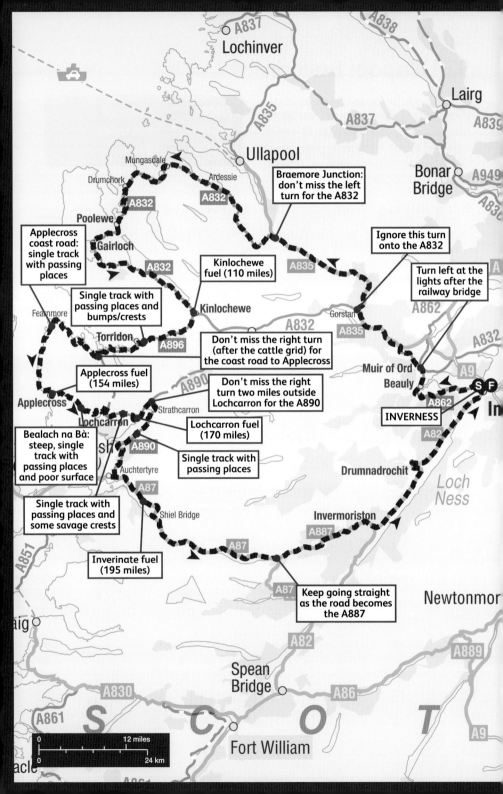

93 West Coast 260

This isn't a short afternoon ride but an alternative to the two-day North Coast 500. It includes the challenging Bealach Na Bà ('Pass of the Cattle') from Applecross and also my favourite road in Scotland, the A87.

FROM	Inverness
DISTANCE	261 miles
ALLOW	A full day

Starting station: BP, 22–24 Longman Road, Inverness IV1 1RY

MILE	LOCATION	TURN	ON	TO	FOR
0	Inverness	↰ ⟳	A82	**Fort William**	0.5
0.5	Inverness	⟲ ⟳	A862	**Beauly**	14.5
15	Muir of Ord	◀🚦	A832	**Ullapool**	5
20	A835 T-junction	↰	A835	**Ullapool**	27.5
47.5	Braemore Jct.	↰	A832	**Gairloch**	62.5
110	Kinlochewe	↱	A896	**Torridon**	18
128	after Shieldaig	↱	minor	**Kenmore**	26
154	Applecross	↰	minor	**Lochcarron**	9
163	A896 T-junction	↱	A896	**Lochcarron**	9
172	A896	↱	A890	**Kyle of Lochalsh**	15
187	A87 T-junction	↰	A87	**Fort William**	45
232	Glenmoriston	↰	A82	**Inverness**	29
261	Inverness				

Northern Ireland

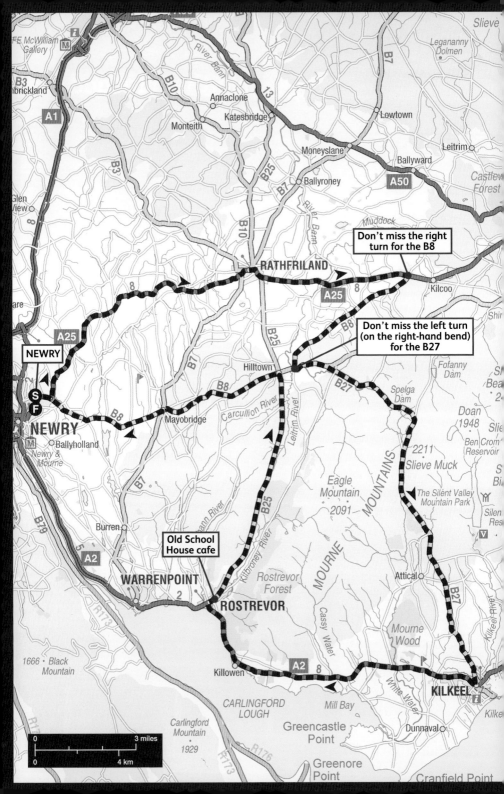

94 Mourne Hourglass

As a visitor to Northern Ireland, it was the riding in the Mourne Mountains that surprised and delighted me the most – so this short route aims to cram in as many miles there as possible.

FROM	Newry
DISTANCE	56 miles
ALLOW	1 hr 25 mins

Starting station: Emo, Dublin Road, Newry BT35 8DA

MILE	LOCATION	TURN	ON	TO	FOR
0	Newry	↰ ↔◇	A25	**Rathfriland**	8.5
8.5	Rathfriland	↱	A25	**Hilltown**	5.5
14	A25	↱	B8	**Hilltown**	4.5
18.5	B8	↰	B27	**Kilkeel**	12.5
31	Kilkeel	↱ 🚦▶	A2	**Newry**	9.5
40.5	Rostrevor	◇▶	B25	**Hilltown**	7
47.5	Hilltown	↰	B8	**Newry**	8.5
56	Newry				

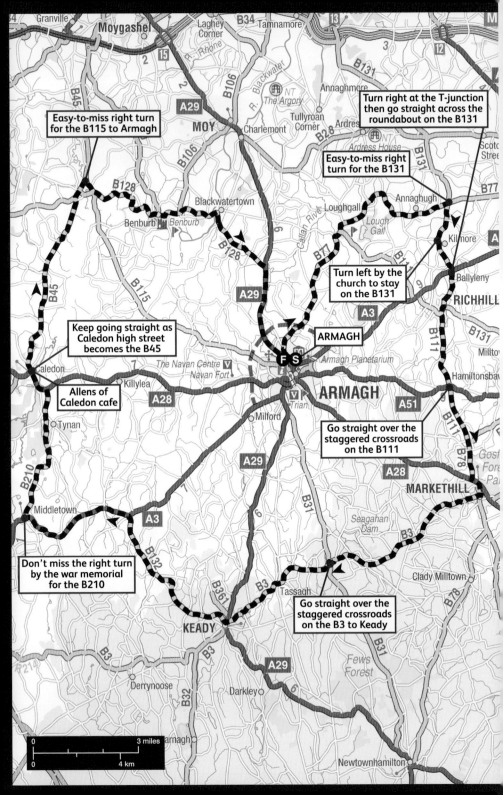

95 Armagh Believer

My friend Damian McAfee helped refine this route through the apple country of South Armagh. His top tip is to watch out for agricultural vehicles in September, when the harvest is on.

FROM	Armagh
DISTANCE	**55 miles**
ALLOW	**1 hr 40 mins**

Starting station: Go, 49 Railway Street, Armagh BT61 7HP

MILE	LOCATION	TURN	ON	TO	FOR
0	Armagh	↱ ⟳	B77	**Loughgall**	8.5
8.5	B77	↱	B131	**Richhill**	3.5
12	Richhill	↔⟳	B111	**Markethill**	4.5
16.5	A28	↰↱	B3	**Markethill**	0.5
17	Markethill	⟳→↔⟳	B3	**Keady**	9.5
26.5	Keady	↰↱	B132	**Middletown**	4.5
31	A3 T-junction	↰	A3	**Middletown**	3.5
34.5	Middletown	↱	B210	**Caledon**	4
38.5	A28 T-junction	↰	A28	**Caledon**	6.5
45	B45	↱	B115	**Armagh**	0.5
45.5	B115	↰	B128	**Benburb**	4.5
50	Blackwatertown	↱	B128	**Armagh**	2
52	A29 T-junction	↱	A29	**Armagh**	3
55	Armagh				

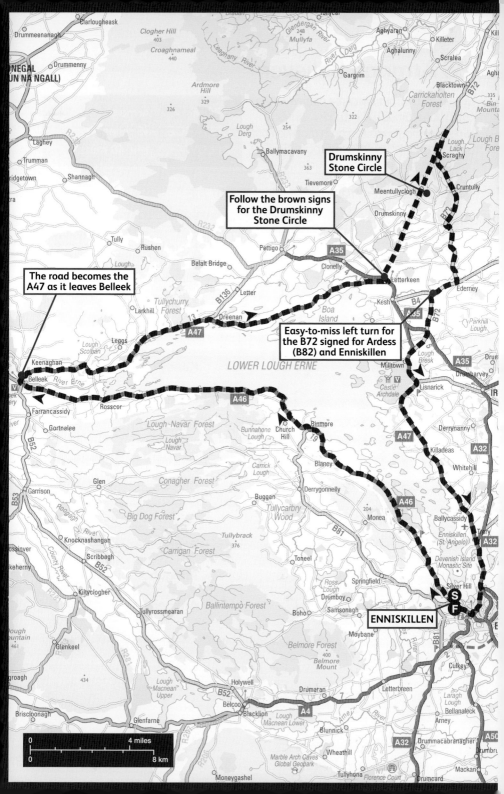

Drumskinny Stone Circle

Follow the brown signs for the Drumskinny Stone Circle

The road becomes the A47 as it leaves Belleek

Easy-to-miss left turn for the B72 signed for Ardess (B82) and Enniskillen

ENNISKILLEN

LOWER LOUGH ERNE

| 0 | | 4 miles |
| 0 | | 8 km |

96 Enniskillen Triangle

This is a short but simple route, broadly following the shores of Lower Lough Erne – though it cuts briefly inland at one point, past the Drumskinny Stone Circle. It's great to have modern roads to such ancient sites.

FROM	Enniskillen
DISTANCE	69 miles
ALLOW	1 hr 30 mins

Starting station: Lilley's Circle K, 27 Lough Shore Road, Enniskillen BT74 5NH

MILE	LOCATION	TURN	ON	TO	FOR
0	Enniskillen	↱	A46	**Belleek**	23
23	Belleek	↱	A52	**Belleek**	16
39	Letterkeen	↰ ↱	minor	**Castlederg**	6.5
45.5	B72 T-junction	↱	B72	**Ederney**	6.5
52	Ederney	⊙→	B4	**Kesh**	1.5
53.5	B4	↰	B82	**Ardess**	2.5
56	A47 T-junction	↰	A47	**Enniskillen**	10.5
66.5	Airport r'bout	⊙	A32	**Enniskillen**	2.5
69	Enniskillen				

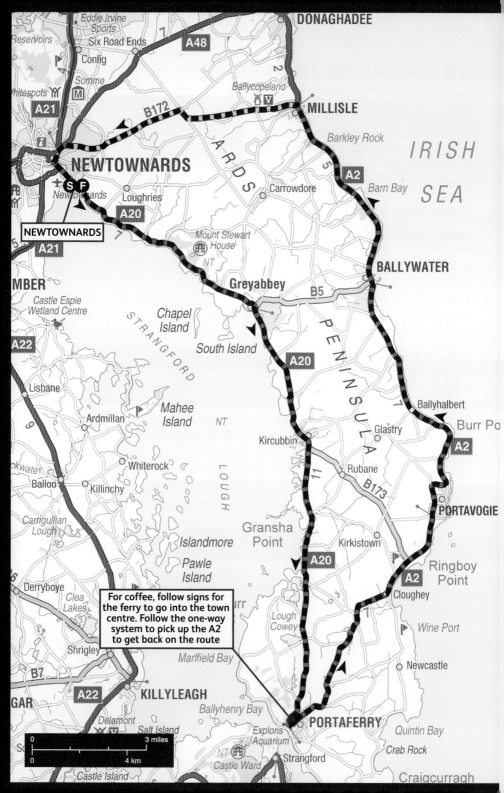

For coffee, follow signs for the ferry to go into the town centre. Follow the one-way system to pick up the A2 to get back on the route

97 Strangford Shores

*A complete lap of Strangford Lough –
using the Portaferry–Strangford crossing
– is a pretty good ride, but I prefer the
views heading back to Newtownards
along the Irish Sea shoreline on this
relaxed route.*

FROM	Newtownards
DISTANCE	**45.5 miles**
ALLOW	**1 hr 15 mins**

Starting station: Strangford Filling Station, 50 Portaferry Road, Newtownards BT23 8SQ

MILE	LOCATION	TURN	ON	TO	FOR
0	Newtownards	↰	A20	**Portaferry**	17.5
17.5	Portaferry	←⟡ ↰	A2	**Cloughey**	20
37.5	Millisle	↰	B172	**Newtownards**	3
40.5	T-junction	↱ ↰	B172	**Newtownards**	5
45.5	Newtownards				

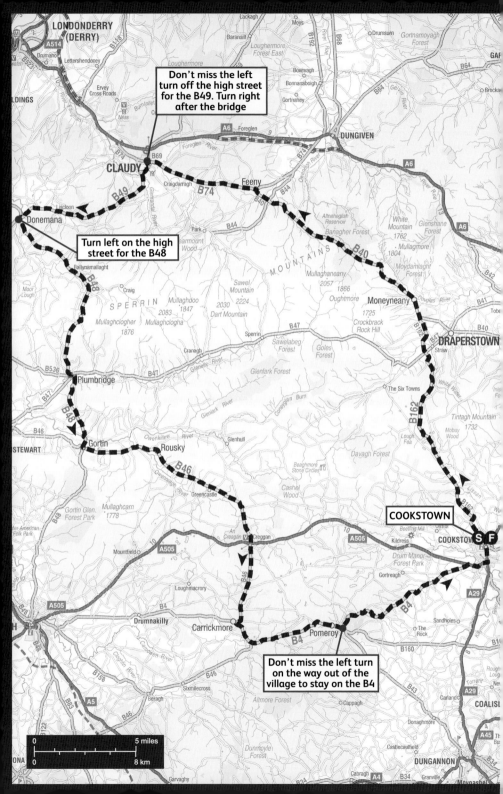

Don't miss the left turn off the high street for the B49. Turn right after the bridge

Turn left on the high street for the B48

Don't miss the left turn on the way out of the village to stay on the B4

COOKSTOWN

98 Cookstown 80

Road racing – especially on a circuit like the Cookstown 100 – takes nerves of steel. You'll be fine with nerves of putty on this far longer road route, which sticks to simple roads (at sensible speeds please) for a laid-back ride.

FROM	Cookstown
DISTANCE	81.5 miles
ALLOW	2 hrs

Starting station: Solo, Lissan Road, Cookstown BT80 8EQ

MILE	LOCATION	TURN	ON	TO	FOR
0	Cookstown	←	B162	**Draperstown**	10.5
10.5	B47 junction	⤴	B40	**Moneyneany**	13
23.5	Feeny	←	B74	**Scenic Route**	5.5
29	Claudy	← ↱	B49	**Donemana**	8
37	Donemana	←	B48	**Plumbridge**	10
47	Plumbridge	← ↱	B48	**Omagh**	4
51	Gortin	←	B46	**Rousky**	10.5
61.5	A505 junction	⬆	B46	**Carrickmore**	4
65.5	Carrickmore	⟳→ ←	B4	**Pomeroy**	6
71.5	Pomeroy	←	B4	**Cookstown**	8
79.5	A505 junction	↱	A505	**Cookstown**	2
81.5	Cookstown				

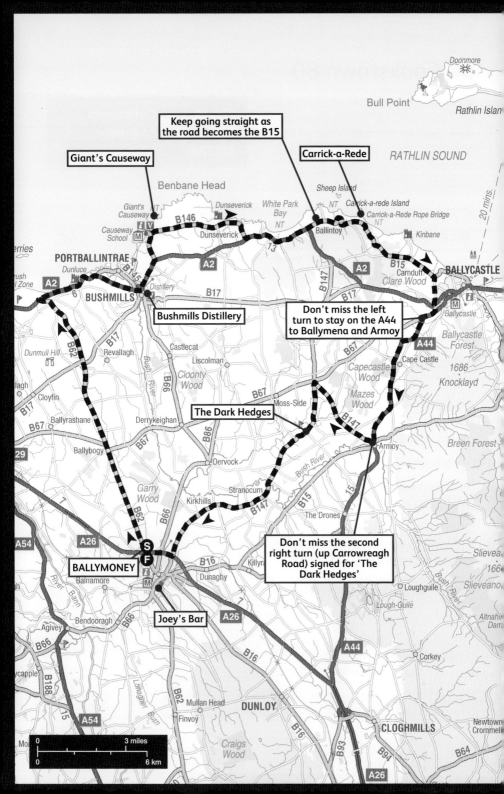

99 Ballymoney Tourist Trail

Biking visitors to Ballymoney have to go to Joey's Bar, once the base of road-racing legend Joey Dunlop. However, this isn't a route for speed but for leisurely pleasure, with a relaxed ride around the tourist hot spots.

FROM	Ballymoney
DISTANCE	46 miles
ALLOW	1 hr 10 mins

Starting station: Maxol, 8 Ballybogey Road, Ballymoney BT53 6QD

MILE	LOCATION	TURN	ON	TO	FOR
0	Ballymoney	↰ ⟳	B62	**Portrush**	9.5
9.5	A2 T-junction	↱	A2	**Bushmills**	4
13.5	Bushmills	↰⟳	A2	**Ballycastle**	1
14.5	A2	↰	B146	**Dunseverick**	4.5
19	T-junction	↰	A2	**Ballycastle**	9
28	Ballycastle	↱↱	A44	**Ballymena**	1
29	A44	↰	A44	**Ballymena**	4.5
33.5	Armoy	↱ ↱	B147	**Ballintoy**	3
36.5	B147 T-junction	↰	B147	**Ballymoney**	9.5
46	Ballymoney				

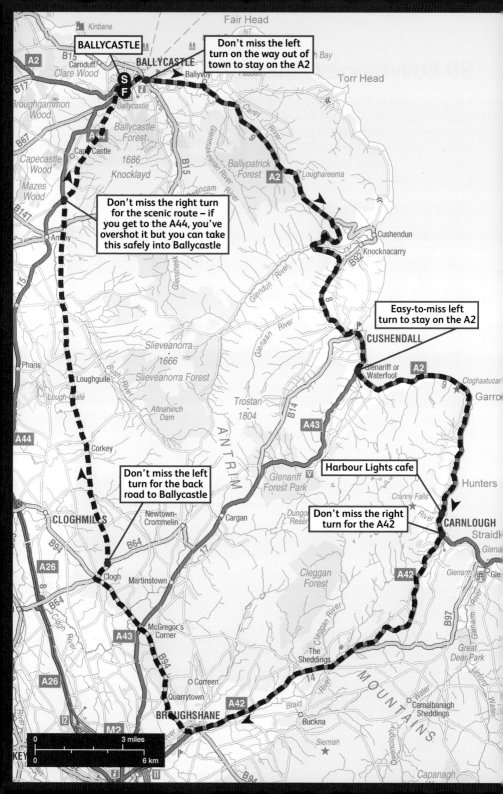

100 Ballycastle Coast Run

The coast road north of Belfast is beautiful... so tourist busses leave the city on it. Riding south from Ballycastle gives better views and a better, bus-free run before looping back to Ballycastle through beautiful countryside.

FROM	**Ballycastle**
DISTANCE	**63 miles**
ALLOW	**1 hr 30 mins**

Starting station: Maxol, Castle Street, Ballycastle BT54 6AR

MILE	LOCATION	TURN	ON	TO	FOR
0	Ballycastle		A2	**Cushendall**	1
1	Ballycastle		A2	**Cushendall**	15
16	Cushendall		A2	**Larne**	1.5
17.5	Waterfoot		A2	**Larne**	9.5
27	Carnlough		A42	**Ballymena**	12
39	Broughshane		B94	**Clough**	4
43	A43 junction		B94	**Clough**	2.5
45.5	Clough		B64	**Newtown-Crommelin**	0.5
46	B64		minor	**Ballycastle**	11.5
57.5	B15 junction		minor	**Scenic Route**	1
58.5	minor road		minor	**Scenic Route**	4.5
63	Ballycastle				

map legend

Motorway	**M1**	Gradient 1:7 (14 %) & steeper	»» »
Motorway Under Construction		Toll	*Toll*
Motorway Proposed		Park & Ride	**P+R**
Motorway Junctions with Numbers	**4**	Mileage between markers	8
Unlimited Interchange	**4** / **4**	Airport	✈
Limited Interchange	**5** / **5**	Airfield	+
Motorway Service Area with access from one carriageway only	**HESTON** Ⓢ Ⓢ	Heliport	Ⓗ
Major Road Service Area with 24 hour facilities	**PEASE POTTAGE** Ⓢ Ⓢ	Ferry (vehicular, sea) (vehicular, river) (foot only)	
Major Road Junctions	Detailed **4**	Railway and Station	
	Other	Level Crossing and Tunnel	
Primary Route	**A12**	River or Canal	
Primary Route Junction with Number	**5**	National Boundary	+ +― +·+
		Built-up Area	
Primary Route Destination	**ENFIELD**	Town, Village or Hamlet	○
Dual Carriageways (A & B roads)		Wooded Area	
Class A Road	**A129**	Spot Height in Feet	813 •
Class B Road	**B177**	Relief above 400' (122m)	
Narrow Major Road (passing places)		Start/finish point	**GLASTONBURY** Ⓢ Ⓕ
Major Roads Under Construction		Direction of travel	▼
Major Roads Proposed		Ferry used en route	

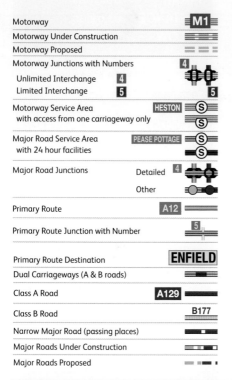

Abbey, Church, Friary, Priory	✝	Garden	✿	Nature Reserve	
Animal Collection		Golf Course	▶	Nature Trail or Forest Walk	
Aquarium		Historic Building	🏛	Picnic Site	⊼
Arboretum, Botanical Garden	♣	Historic Building with Garden		Place of Interest	*Craft Centre* •
Aviary, Bird Garden		Horse Racecourse		Prehistoric Monument	
Battle Site and Date	1066 ⚔	Industrial Monument	☼	Railway, Steam	
Blue Flag Beach		Leisure Park, Leisure Pool		Roman Remains	
Bridge		Lighthouse	🗼	Theme Park	
Castle	🏰	Mine, Cave		Tourist Information Centre	🇮
Castle with Garden		Monument	⚲	Viewpoint (360 degrees)	☀
Cathedral	✝	Motor Racing Circuit		(180 degrees)	
Cidermaker		Museum, Art Gallery	**M**	Vineyard	
Country Park		National Park		Visitor Information Centre	**V**
Distillery		National Trust Property		Wildlife Park	
Farm Park, Open Farm				Windmill	
Fortress, Hill Fort	❈	Natural Attraction	★	Zoo or Safari Park	